A COMMON SENSE
ROAD MAP TO
UNCOMMON WEALTH

A COMMON SENSE ROAD MAP TO UNCOMMON WEALTH

The Key to Achieving Financial Success

MARVIN H. DONIGER

iUniverse, Inc.
New York   Bloomington   Shanghai

A Common Sense Road Map To Uncommon Wealth
The Key to Achieving Financial Success

iUniverse books may be ordered through booksellers or by contacting:

iUniverse
1663 Liberty Drive
Bloomington, IN 47403
www.iuniverse.com
1-800-Authors (1-800-288-4677)

Because of the dynamic nature of the Internet, any Web addresses or links contained in this book may have changed since publication and may no longer be valid.

The information, ideas, and suggestions in this book are not intended to render professional advice. Before following any suggestions contained in this book, you should consult your personal accountant or other financial advisor. Neither the author nor the publisher shall be liable or responsible for any loss or damage allegedly arising as a consequence of your use or application of any information or suggestions in this book.

ISBN: 978-0-595-48465-2 (pbk)
ISBN: 978-0-595-60557-6 (ebk)

Printed in the United States of America

CONTENTS

SECTION I

INTRODUCTION

Recent events in my life have caused me to reflect on my life and the lessons that I want to impart to my two wonderful daughters whom I love dearly, to my grandchildren who have allowed me to stop and sniff the roses along the path of life, and most of all to my adoring, supportive wife who has always been there for me when I have needed her the most. Unfortunately, my pursuit of life has caused me to not enjoy my children during their formative years as much as I would have liked. Despite this, they have become adults of whom I beam with pride. This has been probably more due to my wife's world class parenting and personal sacrifices than to any minor contributions that I might have made. Through the environment that my wife and I created for our daughters, they were able to obtain college educations and achieve successes in their chosen fields of endeavor.

It is my firm belief that grandchildren allow grandparents a second chance to watch a child's progression, share in their triumphs, and share unconditional, reciprocal love with them. As I watch my grandchildren's progress, I reflect on the journey they are taking and the steps in the journey of life that I have taken so far. As I approach the sunset of my life, I have the time and understanding of the importance of watching the sunrise of their lives.

A few years ago, my life's journey took an unexpected detour. Some of the decisions that I made early in my life helped mitigate the impact of my unfortunate circumstances. Together with my wife as my partner, we have, in some cases consciously and in other cases unconsciously, made a series of decisions that have allowed us to reach our present situation. We have sacrificed short term gratification in order to enjoy longer term, more lasting goals. As we faced the inevitable challenges of life, our willingness to discipline ourselves has allowed us to successfully overcome them.

While I do not believe that our life's journey is typical, I also do not believe that it is atypical. Everyone faces challenges.

Most Americans are unprepared to face the financial challenges that they will almost certainly encounter during their lifetimes. In 2006, their savings rate (-0.5 percent) was the lowest since the depths of the Great Depression. In 2005, 39 percent of those within ten years of retirement had less than $25,000 in retirement savings. These statistics are particularly disturbing when one considers that the Baby Boomers were influenced by the sacrifices of their parents who lived through

World War II and/or the Great Depression. If their savings rate is so woefully inadequate, one cannot be optimistic about the prospects for the savings habits of their children.

Many of today's youth have access to guidance counselors who can advise them on what courses to take to prepare for college. What is woefully lacking is a source of information on how to maximize one's career potential and to develop a plan for accumulating wealth. Many of those graduating from college do not have either a career or a savings road map. It is these adolescents and young adults for whom this book has been written. It is also a tool for their parents and counselors to assist them in planning for their futures.

This book is divided into two sections. The first section of this book describes:

- How one develops from a child to an adult and the attributes one obtains in this process. Traits that are developed during this process greatly influence the careers that are chosen and the savings habits that are developed.
- Three strategies for saving for retirement. The recent trend of companies eliminating pensions and health care benefits for their retirees places responsibility for these benefits squarely on the individual.
- Trends in outsourcing, pensions, labor unions, etc. that affect one's career and retirement. Despite the common perception, many of these trends have been occurring for hundreds of years. In fact, much of the improvement in living standards can be directly attributed to Globalization and Innovation, two issues that many perceive to be threats not opportunities.
- Finally this section concludes with a series of key takeaways.

The second section of this book provides:

- A discussion of the impact of inflation on the purchasing power of our wealth and the relative merits of various investment alternatives.
- Detailed road maps for implementing the three retirement strategies discussed in Section I.
- Descriptions of the various terminologies associated with investing. Their purpose is to expose the reader to the terminology of investing.
- Guidelines to be used in developing one's own specific investment strategies.
- A series of key takeaways of the concepts presented in this section
- Summary of the key concepts discussed in this book.

THE JOURNEY CALLED LIFE

All of us are destined to progress through the inevitable journey called life. As we do so, decisions that are made both for us and by us will profoundly impact the experience. After conception, the mother makes decisions that can impact the health of her child. Should the mother smoke, drink, or use drugs, the baby's health could be compromised. The caring mother, knowing that her influence on her child has just begun, will seek the proper medical care and follow a dietary and life style that will promote the proper environment for her child to flourish in her womb. She will discipline herself to not merely prevent harm to the child but to make the necessary sacrifices to ensure her child's health and general well being.

Life's Progression

At birth, the child begins an evolutionary process. The newborn begins the transition from the protected world of his or her mother's womb to the world outside with its numerous obstacles and opportunities. It has been observed that life can be broken down into a series of stages and phases within each stage. The following chart is based on the work of Harlan Gilbert, Bernard Lievegoed, George O'Neill, Rudolph Treichler, and Rudolph Steiner. The chart of Life's Progression describes the development that occurs in seven year increments.

During the three phases of Childhood, we develop the physical and cognitive functions that make each of us unique. Many of our interests that we will pursue in later life are formed. These interests may guide us to seek further education, pursue a career in sports or entertainment, enter the workforce, or become an entrepreneur. Also, our proclivity for saving is influenced by the behavior of our parents. As we reach the end of our childhood, most of us will also have become self sufficient.

LIFE'S PROGRESSION		
STAGE/Phase	Age	Description
CHILDHOOD		This is the stage that is characterized by a shift from total dependency on others towards self awareness and self sufficiency,
Conception— Infancy	0	• Life begins • Child begins his/her physical and cognitive development
Early Childhood	7	• Body undergoes its most important growth phases • Sensory perception develops • Learning occurs through imitation of the environment and activity
Elementary School	14	• Child achieves most of his/her adult height • Forces that cause growth metamorphose into the capacity for learning
Adolescence	21	• Body reaches ultimate growth • Abstract reasoning and rational judgments develop • Strong inner life arises, including personal feelings

Young Adulthood is when we refine our sense of who we are, bring stability to our lives, refine our careers and develop our economic well being. It is at this time that we will incur many of the most significant obligations of our lives. We transition from being responsible for are own being to providing for others. We marry, purchase homes, and have children. In addition to the need to clothe and feed our families, we must also pay our mortgages and should save for college and our retirement. We must wisely make trade-offs between current consumption and investments in the future well being of our family. In addition, we face potential financial crises due to loss of job, medical emergencies, or the need to provide assistance to our parents. While at this stage of our lives the chances of these events happening are low, we cannot totally ignore them. Consideration should be given to formalizing the plans that we have made for our careers and investments and establishing baselines against which our progress can be objectively measured.

LIFE'S PROGRESSION		
STAGE/Phase	Age	Description
YOUNG ADULTHOOD		During this stage much of the development takes place through interactions with others
Phase I	28	The first phase is one of exploration • Soul experiences felt intensely • Different options tested out as the young adult finds his/her feet • Young adult led by the environment and its possibilities
Phase II	35	The second phase involves settling down and organizing: • Life usually becomes more internalized and stable • Period of increasing self-direction and commitment
Phase III	42	The third phase is one of consolidation and reflection

Middle Age involves the recognition of our limitations and the refinement of our life's goals. As we progress in our chosen field of endeavor, we develop a set of skills and capabilities for which the market has an established demand. At this point in our careers, potential employers are interested in individuals who have proven that they can meet the requirements of the position not those who might have the potential. It is at this juncture in our lives, that we become more aware of the deterioration of our health. In fact, many of us may face our first serious illnesses. By this point in our lives, we have started the transition from anticipating the future to reflecting on our past. For most of us, some of our financial obligations, such as raising our children, have been satisfied while others, such as providing for our retirement still remain ahead of us. Whether we divert the financial resources we invested in our children to our retirement or to our current standard of living will be critical in determining the quality of our old age. Will we be able to afford to satisfy our needs or will we have to make dramatic sacrifices in our life styles?

LIFE'S PROGRESSION		
STAGE/Phase	**Age**	**Description**
MIDDLE AGE		Development more dependent upon individual intitiative, less upon others.
Phase I	49	The first phase involves acceptance of limitations (physical, career, personality, etc.). New directions may open up.
Phase II	56	The second phase is an expansion of the intitiatives in phase one
Phase III	63	The third phase focuses on concluding life's work and preparing for retirement and old age

Old Age can be golden years if we have lived a healthy lifestyle and prepared wisely for our retirement. This is the time when the decisions that we either consciously or subconsciously made can be evaluated. If we made good decisions, then we can reap the rewards of those decisions and the sacrifices that we might have made. If our decisions were wrong then we must suffer the consequences. At this stage of our lives, it becomes virtually impossible to finance the remainder of our lives unless we had prepared wisely and diligently earlier in life.

LIFE'S PROGRESSION		
STAGE/Phase	**Age**	**Description**
OLD AGE		This final stage imvolves: • Enjoying grandchildren • Reflecting on one's legacy • Accelerating deterioration of faculties • Losing independence and self sufficiency • Accepting the inevitable

Career Strategies

In developing our life's strategy, either consciously or subconsciously, we can choose two different paths. The first path is a broad one that allows us to maximize the opportunities in our lives. In it we choose to broaden our skills, perspectives and experiences. More often than not, this is a result of our parents stressing the importance of education, development of interpersonal skills, appreciation of the arts and participation in sports. The second path is a more focused strategy, where at a relatively early age we identify our life's ambition and pursue it as vigorously as we can. The following diagram depicts these two strategies in terms of Life's Progression.

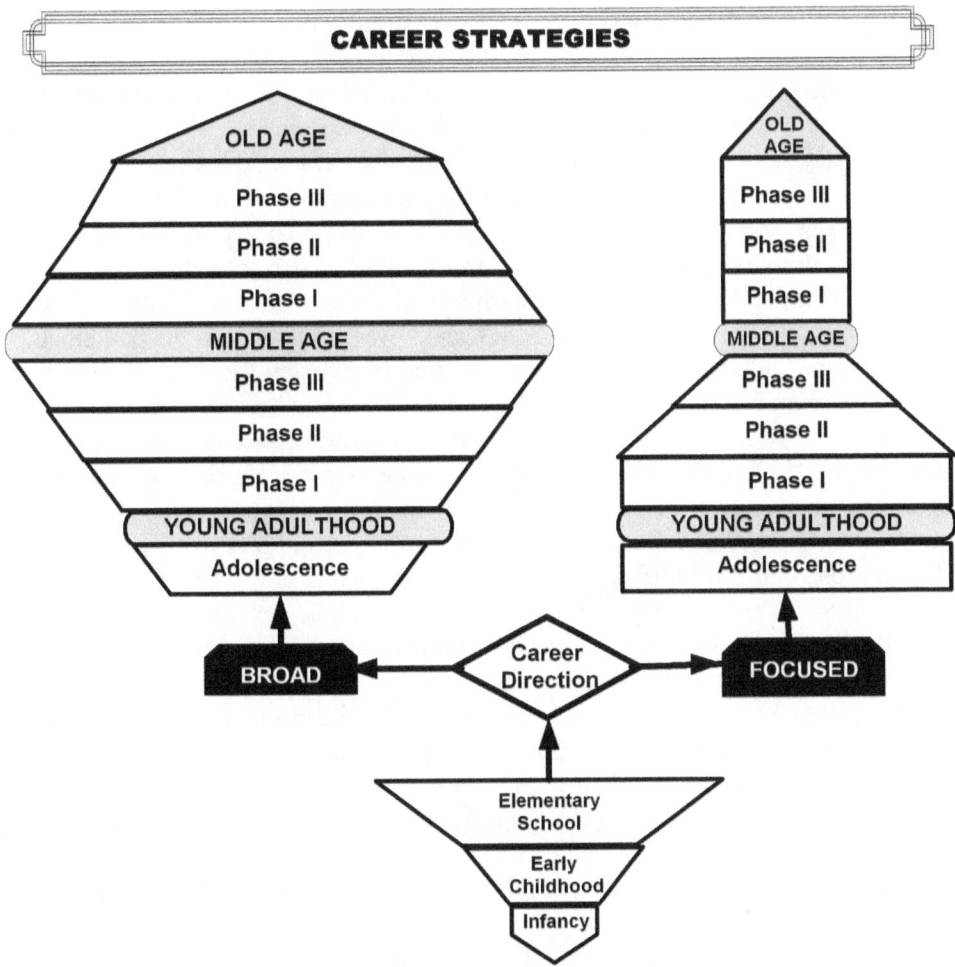

From Infancy through Elementary School, parents set the framework for their children to develop their individuality and the disciplines to achieve their life's ambitions. They celebrate their children's accomplishments and are supportive in times of disappointment. Sometime before graduating from high school, choices regarding the direction that his/her life will take must be made by the child, who has by now become an adolescent, in conjunction with inputs from his/her parents, teachers and others. This is a critical juncture in positioning the child-adolescent to capitalize on the career opportunities that he/she will be able to pursue during his/her life. Since most children at this stage of their lives don't have a clear sense of the direction they wish to pursue, they should follow a strategy that will not restrict the range of opportunities that will be available to them.

The risks of pursuing an ill conceived career strategy that is focused on achieving an improbable objective must be thoroughly understood. The chances of someone succeeding as a professional athlete or entertainer are exceedingly small. Of those few who actually do succeed, most of their careers are very short. Many professional athletes' careers are over by the time they reach 30 because of injury or deteriorating physical abilities; entertainers' success can be limited to one song, movie or television appearance. If they have not developed other skills, then their career options in other fields of endeavor are very limited. An athlete who excelled beyond sports is Bill Bradley, a scholar athlete, who was a Rhodes Scholar, played ten seasons in the NBA for the New York Knicks, was inducted into the Basketball Hall of Fame, and served as the US Senator from New Jersey. On the other hand, those who know at this stage in their life that they want to become a doctor, lawyer, teacher or other professional can pursue a long and successful career in their chosen field of interest provided that they continue to match the continued development of their skills with the evolving requirements of their profession. They do not reach any physical or intellectual limitations in their ability to practice their chosen profession until Old Age. In certain fields such as engineering, medicine, and computers, technology is advancing at such a rapid rate that within a few years the knowledge acquired in college becomes obsolete. Those that do not continue to develop their skills face the same fate as the athlete or entertainer.

The goal of a broad career strategy is to maximize the number of career opportunities that will be available throughout ones professional career. Those pursuing this course of action should identify the career paths that are of interest to them, ensure that they have acquired the requisite educational background, and start their job career in an industry and company that will provide them with the requisite skills, experiences and opportunities for advancement consistent with their long term career objectives.

Throughout their crucial career development during the Young Adulthood Stage, those that achieve success demonstrate an ability to accomplish things of significance, expand their horizons, and assume a leadership role in the success of the organization in which they work. Getting the necessary experience, may require them to relocate, change companies or industries, and even accept a position with lesser compensation. Just as they invest the time, energy, and money to succeed academically, they must invest in their career development wherever the appropriate opportunity may exist. This may require sacrifices for them and their families. Each one must decide for themselves the importance of their professional and personal lives and strike the appropriate balance between them.

As they approach Middle Age, they will have twenty or so years of well rounded experience in multiple industries and job functions and not twenty years of having done the same thing. The further into Middle Age one is, the more difficult it is to get an opportunity in a field in which one has limited experience. There are several reasons for this but suffice it to say that potential employers are unwilling to train mature relatively high priced employees. One should keep in mind that when you least expect it and can least react to it life will throw you one heck of a curveball. At one or more times in most people's careers something will occur that impedes their career ambitions. Those with the broader their proven capability, are better equipped to overcome the challenge. By the time one reaches Middle Age, the emphasis has changed from what you can learn from a job opportunity to what can you contribute to the organization. Organizations expect results and have little tolerance for those who do not meet their expectations from the outset.

Retirement Strategies

Until the end of the twentieth century developing a strategy for retirement was not necessary for most people. In 1901, the life expectancy at birth in the United States was forty nine years. At the end of the century it was seventy seven years. The increased longevity in itself was not a problem because many people were covered by defined benefit retirement plans that rewarded employees for their longevity with a company. What created the need for retirement strategies was the migration from defined benefit to defined contribution plans in which the individual became responsible for his/her own retirement. Instead of a company guaranteeing to pay an employee a fixed amount at retirement based on years of service and earnings, it changed to promising to contribute a certain amount to a retirement account to which the employee also contributed. In addition, many companies have reduced or eliminated health insurance coverage for retired employees and even current employees.

Another reason for having a retirement strategy is to create a safeguard to be used in an emergency. One cannot always predict when there will be an emergency that results in an unforeseen expenditure. One cannot foresee a medical condition that can prematurely end a person's ability to earn a living. The following chart shows three strategies for saving for retirement. As will be discussed, the longer one has to invest for retirement the less risk one has to incur. The converse is also true. The longer one waits to save for retirement, the more risk one must assume. The longer one waits to save enough money for retirement the longer one may have to work. In the extreme case, a person may have to work forever or become a burden on his/her family or society. There is much evidence to suggest that a great many people have not saved enough money for their retirement.

According to a 2004 Survey of Consumer Finances by the Federal Reserve Board, 47.9 percent of workers under the age of sixty five were covered by either a defined benefit or contribution retirement plan. That same survey found that in 2004 the median value of all retirement accounts owned by households headed by persons between the ages of fifty five and sixty four was $88,000. This is an amount that would allow a sixty five year old person in May, 2006 to purchase a level, single-life annuity that would replace only 15 percent of the median income of $53,500 among households headed by individuals of that same age group in 2004.

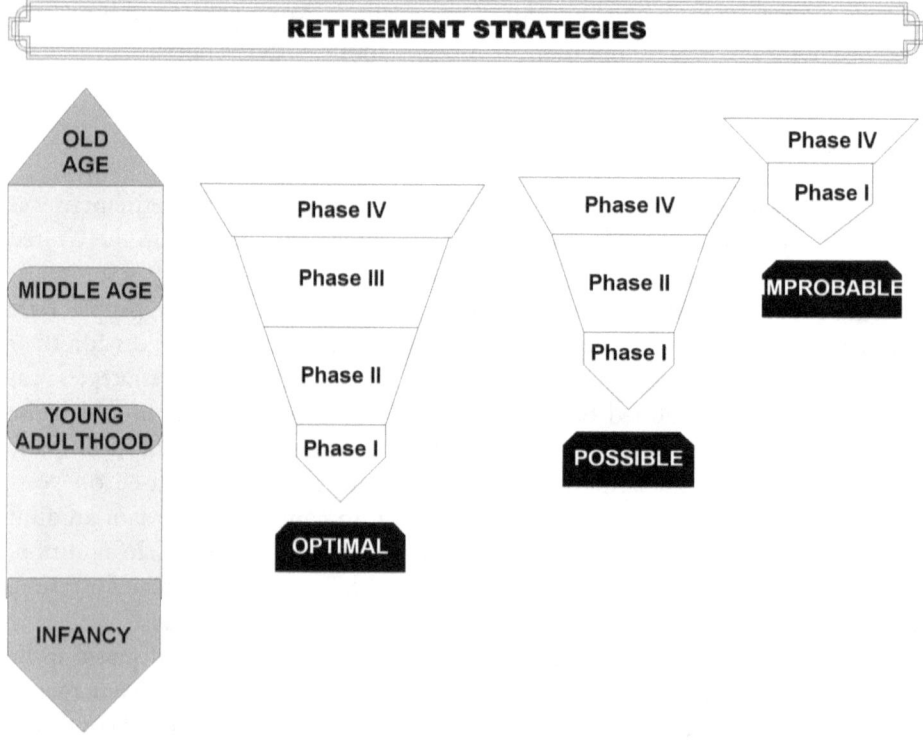

RETIREMENT STRATEGIES

Under the Optimal Retirement Strategy, one would start saving for retirement before reaching the Young Adulthood Stage of Life's Progression. If one started his/her retirement savings program at age twenty five, he/she would have forty years to save for retirement. Under the assumption that at retirement the retiree earned the median income of $53,500 and wished to replace all of his/her pre-retirement income, that person would need approximately $865,000 at retirement. In order to have saved that amount, one would have had to save $4,625 per year for forty years and earned a return on investment of 5 percent per year. If one were able to receive an annual return of 7.5 percent per year over forty years, one would have to save $2,400 per year; a 10 percent annual return would require saving $1,205 per year. At a 5 percent annual return, it would require saving over 8.5 percent of pre-tax income per year to save enough to replace 100 percent of pre-retirement income. One could decide to reduce the amount saved per year by taking on more risk in order to achieve higher returns, adjusting expectations of one's retirement standard of living to reflect a reduced retirement income stream, delaying retirement, or a combination of these options. However, in planning for retirement there is no reason to believe that over a forty year period that the average annual returns would not be between 5 percent and 10 percent.

In the Possible Retirement Strategy, one would start at Phase II of the Young Adulthood Stage or thirty five years of age and save thirty years for retirement. Under this strategy one would have to save $8,405 per year with a 5 percent average annual return on investment; $5,275 per year with a 7.5 percent return; or $3,240 with a 10 percent average annual return. This strategy would require making more drastic trade-offs between current consumption and saving for retirement. Many people will be forced into this strategy because of their need to feed, clothe and shelter their families and to finance their children's college education. They may be required, just as under the Optimal Strategy to alter their assumptions regarding rates of return, standard of retirement living and/or postponing retirement. With discipline this approach can work.

In the Improbable Retirement Strategy, "The What Me Worry Generation" does not start until they are in the latter part of the Middle Age Stage or fifty six years of age. At this point, one has only ten years to save for retirement. Those individuals who have procrastinated in preparing for retirement face unpalatable alternatives. They can try to save $44,400 per year that would earn 5 percent, $38,500 at 7.5 percent, or $33,450 at 10 percent; postpone their retirement age; or drastically reduce their retirement standard of living. While over a thirty or forty year period, one could expect to receive a return on one's investment of 5 percent to 10 percent per year, over a ten year period one would have less certainty in estimating potential returns on an investment. The risks of trying to achieve historically high rates of return should not be undertaken as there is no time to recoup any loses that might be sustained. One could rationalize all the reasons for not having saved for retirement but none of them will solve the quagmire of not adequately preparing for retirement. To be realistic, individuals who find themselves in this situation must continue to work and save as much as they can and postpone their retirement. If they are unable to work in their old age, the alternatives are even more limited and unpalatable.

Old Age reduces the range of activities that we can pursue. The deterioration of our health forces us to increase our spending on various kinds of health care. Facing one's mortality is difficult enough. Doing it without adequate source of income is an even more daunting challenge

THE INEVITABILITY OF CHANGE

Change is inevitable and one must adapt in order to not merely survive but to prosper. Those institutions, as well as individuals, that accept that change is inevitable and successfully embrace and adapt can flourish; those that do not, run the risk of stagnation, deterioration or even extinction. Every change presents unique sets of opportunities, as well as risks, to that which are affected by it. This is true whether a government, a company, or an individual is affected. Ignore the winds of change; suffer the consequences. The sooner that a change is foreseen and its implications understood, the sooner it can be capitalized on. Protecting the *status quo* can be a strategy for disaster.

In the year 2008, the United States faces numerous challenges. Some would even say that these challenges are unprecedented.

- Terrorism has struck the United States with an unmerciful vengeance and caused the very foundation of the American way of life to undergo a metamorphosis that was unimaginable before the fateful events of Sept 11, 2001. As a result, it has become necessary to balance individual liberties against the collective need for security.

- Hurricanes of epic proportions have hit the Gulf Coast. The City of New Orleans has been devastated and tens of thousands of its residents have suffered greatly.

- Government budgets have gone from surplus to mammoth deficits as the Federal Government stimulated the economy through fiscal policy and the most accommodative monetary policy in memory. In addition, "The War on Terror," expanded health care coverage for seniors, reconstruction efforts for those affected by hurricanes Katrina and Rita caused spending to explode. While these crises have occurred, the politicians in Washington have continued their legacy of feeding at the trough of pork barrel and corruption. They exhibit a propensity to spend frivolously while failing to address looming crises such as the projected deficits of Social Security and Medicare. They have no incentive whatsoever to make the hard choices. They continually reward their constituents who re-elect them and leave the ultimate costs and sacrifices to future generations.

- America faces its second energy crisis in the last thirty years. In the 1970s disruptions in supply caused the crisis. Now the crisis has been caused by exploding demand in the developing countries, most notably China and India, failures to invest in exploration and refining capacity, excessive governmental regulations that constrain supply and increase prices, and fears of disruption in the supply of oil from unstable countries.

- Competition from developing countries with economic advantages that some consider unfair is inevitable. American industry is faced with many challenges in this world of globalization, the possibility of terrorist acts against facilities around the world, foreign government subsidies, shortages of people with the skills requirements of the twenty-first century, exclusion from foreign markets, limited pricing power, etc. Companies are not the only ones with challenges. Workers face the loss of jobs to lower cost workers elsewhere in the world; retirees' pensions and healthcare benefits are being curtailed; income growth has failed to keep up with the cost of living; and the dream of improving lifestyles for their children has been jeopardized.

If history is any guide, despite the current concerns there is reason for optimism. This optimism can be justified based on the spirit of the American people and the economic system called capitalism.

- The United States in its short history has overcome the devastation of a Civil War, two World Wars, the Cold War, as well as the Korean and Vietnam wars and many other crises. It was attacked at Pearl Harbor and responded to that incursion on our peace with the sacrifices of its people and its ability to adapt. It led the liberation of Europe and, through the Marshall Plan, the reconstruction of Europe.
- Natural Disasters of epic proportions are not new to the United States. The City of San Francisco was destroyed in 1906, Florida and the Gulf Coast suffered devastation from numerous hurricanes, and drought struck the country's breadbasket. Yet the American people faced these challenges and prospered.
- Hopefully sooner rather than later, as they have in the past, our leaders will have the courage to make the difficult decisions regarding Governmental spending and regulations that can keep the American economy the most vibrant in the world. Succumbing to the political pressures of special interest groups who want to perpetuate the unsustainable *status quo* could relegate the United States to stagnation and a reduction in the standard of living of its people. Were this to happen, it is possible that this country could suffer the malaise of France, Germany and other European countries where economic growth is stagnant, productivity growth anemic, unemployment rampant and the demands on government for services unsupportable by economic realities.

- Foreign competition, or Globalization, is often mentioned by the media and politicians as a new phenomenon and a threat to the American way of life. It is not only not new but it also not a source of despair; it can be a phenomenal opportunity.

The rest of this chapter will discuss the evolution of Globalization, the Industrial Revolution, the Labor Unions, and Capitalism and their implications for our lives and investments.

Globalization

First of all, let me state that Globalization is not a new concept nor is it necessarily a threat. Its basis can be traced to some writings on this subject that go back to the latter part of the 18th and the first part of the 19th centuries.

In 1776, in *An Inquiry into the Nature and Causes of the Wealth of Nations* by Adam Smith, the concept of comparative advantage was discussed. His thesis can be summarized as follows:

Outputs produced by a nation are either consumed by it or used to exchange for the outputs of others. Its wealth is based on the relationship between what is produced and what is consumed. This relationship is determined by the effectiveness with which its resources are utilized and the proportion of resources that are utilized for productive purposes as compared to those resources that are not. This effectiveness is a function of the capital that is invested in these resources. Countries tend to implement policies and allocate capital in investments that favor certain industries. *"Since the downfall of the Roman empire, the policy of Europe has been more favourable to arts, manufactures, and commerce, the industry of towns, than to agriculture, the industry of the country."*

In 1817, David Ricardo expounded on the "Theory of Comparative Advantage" in his book, *The Principles of Political Economy and Taxation*. Basically, he theorized that:

It would be in the best interests of a nation to specialize in producing those goods or services in which it had a cost advantage and trade with those nations for goods and services in which they had a relative cost advantage.

Thus the notion of trade and the worldwide allocation of resources, such as capital and labor, are based on the effective investment of excess capital in those nations that can most productively utilize it. Those nations who produced more than they consumed would be the source of investments that could be made in those nations that could most effectively utilize that excess capital. While the concept of wealth and comparative advantage, were initially applied to nations, they also apply to businesses within those nations. Businesses should invest where they can maximize the return on capital to its owners. In order to achieve this, the capital should be deployed irrespective of location. This may mean its own facilities or those of another company, either through acquisition or partnership, in some other city, state, or country. The implications of this are that capital, without external influences, such as government regulations, should flow to where investment returns can be maximized.

Modern Innovation Revolution

Since its inception, the United States has been able to effectively capitalize on various innovations developed here and elsewhere, primarily Europe. Whether its has been due to its bountiful resources, the ingenuity of its people, the good fortune to be building its economy and its infrastructure at a time of acclerating innovation, or by sheer luck, no one can say for certain. Irrespective of the cause, the effect on it has been quite remarkable.

During the latter part of the 18th and beginning of the 19th centuries, innovations such as the steam engine and the cotton gin, allowed the United States to improve its rural agrcultural economy and begin its migration to a more urban, manufacturing based economy. The steam locomotive and steamboat allowed it to move its products further and more efficently.

As the nineteenth century evolved, developments in communications, such as the telegraph, trans Atlantic cable, telephone, and the wireless telgraph, allowed information to be shared over longer distances in shorter timespans. Instead of days, weeks, or months, information could be sent hundreds of miles in minutes. Manufacturing developed new capabilities, such as the internal combustion and diesel engines, the Bessemer process for making steel, and the ability to refine gasoline. Man was able to build more complex structures, the first skyscraper (a ten story building in Chicago) and the Brooklyn Bridge (the largest suspension bridge in the world at that time and the first steel-wire suspension bridge) in the United States and the Eiffel Tower (the tallest structure in the world when its was completed in 1889) in France. During this time period, pasteurization and the aspirin increased life expectancies while the light bulb and phonograph improved the quality of life.

While the eighteenth and especially the nineteenth centuries were blessed with many innovations, they pale in comparison to the achievements of the twentieth century. Developments such as the vacuum diode, triode, radio tuner, cathode ray tube, transistor and the fiber optic cable allowed dramatic improvements in the ability to communicate farther, faster and cheaper. The automobile, airplane and jet engine dramatically improved the mobilty of man and goods. As the century evolved, it became possible to travel farther in much less time and at a significantly lower cost. Globalization could not have evolved without these improvements in communications and transportation. It became profitable to transfer activities from high cost countries to those more cost effective ones located thousands of miles away. Initially it was manufacturing activites. But at the end of the century, it became knowledge based activities such as call centers, accounting tasks, engineering, and software development.

During the twentieth century, discoveries of Insulin, the iron lung, penicillin, the kidney dialysis machine, synthetic cortisone, antibiotics, the Salk Polio vaccine, the internal pacemaker, gene splicing and the artificial heart, dramtaically increased life expectancies. In fact, the life expectancy for someone born at the end of the twentieth century had increased to 77 years from 49 years at the start of the century. The modern escalator, safety razor, vacuum cleaner, air conditioner, frozen food, microwave oven, etc., made life easier. New industries developed around innovations that made entertainment available to millions of people around the world who had more leisure time. These innovations included movie pictures, technicolor, radio, television, stereo records along with audio and video recorders as well as the digital video recorder.

Perhaps one of the most important innovations during this century occurred in the field of computing. The genesis of the modern computer can be attributed to the development of the analytic computer in 1834. one hundred years later, in 1934 the analog computer was invented. During the remainder of the twentieth century, a series of developments produced advancements in computing that have made vast computation capabilities available at minimal costs. These developments occurred as a result of revolutions in the design of computers and the techniques for manufacturing them.

The following table highlights many of the key innovations that inexcorably affected the quality of life of people around the world. In reviewing these innovations, one cannot help but be in awe of the innovations of the twentieth century as compared to the preceeding century and a quarter.

225 YEARS of INNOVATION			
18th and 19th Centuries		20th Century	
Year	Invention	Year	Invention
1775	First efficient steam engine	1900	Zeppelin
1793	Cotton gin		Modern escalator
1801	Steam locomotive	1901	Safety razor
1807	Steamboat		Radio receiver
1834	Analytic engine (forerunner of the computer)		Vacuum cleaner
	Photography	1902	Air conditioner
1837	Telegraph		Neon light
1846	Pneumatic tire	1903	First powered flight.
1849	Reinforced concrete.	1904	Vacuum diode
1850	Gasoline refining	1906	Sonar
1851	Sewing machine.		Triode
1854	Bessemer Steel Process	1907	First synthetic plastic
1858	Trans-Atlantic cable		Color photography
1859	Internal combustion engine	1908	Gyrocompass
1862	Pasteurization		Cellophane
1867	Dynamite		Model T Ford
1873	Typewriter		Geiger counter
1876	Telephone.	1909	Instant coffee
1877	Phonograph.	1910	Talking motion picture
1878	Microphone		Neon lamp
1879	Incandescent lamp.	1911	Automobile electrical ignition
1883	Skyscraper	1912	Motorized movie cameras
	Brooklyn Bridge		First tank

225 YEARS of INNOVATION			
18th and 19th Centuries		20th Century	
Year	Invention	Year	Invention
1884	Machine gun	1915	Pyrex
1885	Internal-combustion engine powered automobile	1916	Radio tuners
1889	Eiffel Tower.		Stainless steel
1892	Diesel engine	1919	Short-wave radio
1895	Cinematography		Flip-flop circuit
1896	Wireless telegraph.		Arc welder
1899	Aspirin	1921	First robot
		1922	Insulin
		1922	3-D movies
		1923	Cathode-ray tube
			Frozen food
		1925	Mechanical television
		1926	Liquid-fueled rockets
		1927	Quartz crystal watch
			Electronic TV system
			Technicolor
			Aerosol can
			Iron lung
		1928	Penicillin
			Electric shaver
		1929	Car radio
		1930	Scotch tape
			Frozen food

225 YEARS of INNOVATION			
18th and 19th Centuries		20th Century	
Year	Invention	Year	Invention
			Neoprene
			Analog computer
			Jet engine
		1931	Electron microscope
		1932	Polaroid photography
			Radio telescope
		1933	FM radio
			Stereo records
		1934	Magnetic tape recorder
		1935	Nylon
			Canned beer
			Radar
		1936	Voice recognition machine
		1937	Photocopier
			Jet engine
		1938	Ball point pen
			Teflon
			Freeze-dried coffee
			Turboprop engine
		1939	Sikorsky helicopter
			Electron microscope
		1940	Color television
		1941	Software controlled computer
			Aerosol spray can
			Nuclear power

225 YEARS of INNOVATION			
18th and 19th Centuries		20th Century	
Year	Invention	Year	Invention
		1942	Electronic digital computer
		1943	Synthetic rubber
			Aqualung
		1944	Kidney dialysis machine
			Synthetic cortisone
		1945	Atomic bomb
		1946	Microwave oven
		1947	Holography
			Mobile phones
			Transistor
		1948	Velcro
		1950	Credit card
		1951	Video tape
		1952	Bar code
			Diet soft drink
			Hydrogen bomb
		1953	Radial tires
			Black box flight recorder
		1954	Oral contraceptives
			Nonstick pans
			Solar cell
		1955	Tetracycline
			Salk vaccine
		1955	Optic fiber
		1956	Computer hard disk

225 YEARS of INNOVATION			
18th and 19th Centuries		**20th Century**	
Year	**Invention**	**Year**	**Invention**
		1958	Modem
			Laser
			Integrated circuit
		1959	Internal pacemaker
			Microchip
			Xerography
		1960	Halogen lamp
		1961	Valium
			Nondairy creamer
		1962	Audio cassette
		1963	Videodisc
		1964	Permanent-press
		1965	Soft contact lenses
			NutraSweet
			Compact disk
			Kevlar
		1967	Handheld calculator
		1968	Computer mouse
			Computer with integrated circuits
			Random access memory
		1969	Arpanet (first internet)
			Artificial heart
			ATM
			Bar-code scanner

225 YEARS of INNOVATION			
18th and 19th Centuries		20th Century	
Year	Invention	Year	Invention
		1970	Daisy wheel printer
			Floppy disk
		1971	Dot Matrix Printer
			Liquid crystal display
			Microprocessor
			VCR
		1972	Word processor
		1973	Gene splicing
			Ethernet
		1975	Laser printer
		1976	Ink jet printer
		1977	MRI
		1978	Spreadsheet
			Artificial heart
		1979	Cellular phones
			Supercomputer
		1980	Hepatitis-B vaccine
		1981	MS-DOS
			Scanning Tunneling microscope
		1982	Genetically engineered human growth hormone
		1984	CD-ROM
			Apple Macintosh
		1985	Microsoft windows

225 YEARS of INNOVATION			
18th and 19th Centuries		20th Century	
Year	Invention	Year	Invention
		1986	High temperature super conductor
			Synthetic skin
			Disposable camera
		1987	Disposable contact lenses
		1988	Digital cellular phone
			Doppler radar
			Prozac
		1989	High-definition television
		1990	World Wide Web
		1991	Digital answering machine
		1992	Smart pill
		1993	Pentium processor
		1994	HIV protease inhibitor
		1995	DVD
		1996	Web TV
		1997	Gas powered fuel cell
		1998	Viagra
		1999	Tekno Bubbles

Source:
http://about.com
http://www.victorianweb.org

While the twenty-first century has just begun, it would not be unreasonable to postulate that this century's innovations will have affects that cannot even be imagined. Just as visions of nuclear powered submarines and man's ability to fly and even travel in space seemed preposterous to our forefathers, so too will tomorrow's innovations be unimanageable to us today. As was the case with computers, many of this century's innovations may be based on those of previous centuries. The forerunner of the computer was the Analytical Engine that was invented in 1834. In 1942 the first digital computer was built. The modern computer can be traced to the IBM 360's appearance in the marketplace in 1964. Listed in the following table are some of the innovations of the first five years of the current century. It is too soon to determine their ramifications, but many of them may prove to be instruments of profound change just as their predecessors have proven to be.

21st CENTURY INNOVATIONS		
Year	Invention	Description
2000	Nomad retinal scanning display	Micro-miniature projector mounted on a tiny chip beams 18 million pixels per second directly on the retina. Nomad transforms the human eye into a TV set, eliminating any interference between eye and image.
	Digital Angel	Tiny transmitter bonded or implanted under the skin, sends a patient's medical information and precise location to a monitoring system via global-positioning satellites (GPS).
	Fluid Sense infusion pump	Implantable and programmable pager-size pump just under the skin of the abdomen in which morphine is stored. A small tube, or catheter, connected to the pump carries the medication to the fluid-filled space surrounding the spinal cord, where pain signals travel on their way to the brain. In response to breakthrough pain, the patient presses a button on a handheld remote that activates the pump

21st CENTURY INNOVATIONS		
Year	Invention	Description
2001	Artificial liver	Two-part chamber—patient's blood on one side, live rabbit cells suspended in a solution on the other—with a semi-permeable membrane in between. As toxins from the blood pass through the membrane, the rabbit cells metabolize them and send the resulting proteins and other good things back to the other side
	AbioCor artificial heart	Softball-size, plastic-and-titanium AbioCor is entirely self-contained, except for a wireless battery pack strapped to the waist
	Fuel cell bike	Fuel-cell technology, which uses pollution-free hydrogen gas to generate an electric current, to drive an electric motor powered bike
	Self-cleaning windows	Glass that is lined with a transparent coating that breaks down dirt (and bird droppings) in the sun
2002	Braille glove	Device that senses its wearer's hand movements and transmits them wirelessly to a tiny handheld monitor, where they appear as words.
	Phone tooth	Device embedded in a molar that receives cell-phone calls. The signals are translated into vibrations that travel from the tooth to the skull to the inner ear
	Nano-tex	Clothing with a special chemical treatment to give them "nanowhiskers" (millions of tiny fibers one hundred-thousandth of an inch long) that help them repel spills.

21st CENTURY INNOVATIONS		
Year	Invention	Description
	Birth control patch	A patch about the size of a matchbook, but as thin as a piece of tape, that delivers the same estrogen and progestin found in a standard birth-control pill. The hormones pass from the patch through the skin and into the bloodstream
	Foveon Camera clip	Image sensor that directly captures color using three pixels hormones pass from the patch through
	Solar tower	A tower 1 km (.62 miles) tall in the middle of a 20,000 acre greenhouse to trap and heat air. The warm air from the greenhouse will rise through the tower as it would through a chimney, turning turbines and generating electricity.
	Virtual keyboard	A glowing red outline of a keyboard is projected on a desk or other flat surface by a laser beam. A sensor monitors the reflection of an infrared light projected on the same spot and determines which "keys" have been struck by the way that reflection changes.
2003	Optical camouflage system	An optical camouflage system that makes anyone wearing a special reflective material seem to disappear
	Flu-Mist	An influenza vaccine administered as a nasal spray.
	Hybrid car	An automobile powered by a combination of gasoline and electricity.

21st CENTURY INNOVATIONS		
Year	Invention	Description
	Infrared fever screening system	Used in public buildings to scan for people with a high temperature from a fever or Sars
2004	Translucent concrete	Based on a matrix of parallel optical glass fibers embedded into the concrete that can transmit light and color from the outside
	Flower sound	Flower bouquets acting as loudspeakers when placed in a special vase that has electronics hidden in the base.
	SonoPrep	A device for delivering medication by sound waves rather than injection.

Source: *Time Magazine Modern Inventions of the Years 2000–2004*

Labor Union Movement

Labor unions have had a profound influence on the lives of millions of workers. For our purposes a labor union will be defined as group of workers organized for the purpose of improving their working conditions. The labor union movement coincided with the transition from an agrarian society to an industrial society that began in the eighteenth century.

A precursor to the modern union in the United States was the American Federation of Labor (AFL) which was founded in 1885 for the purpose of improving working hours, wages and safety conditions for its members. During the nineteenth century, the labor movement in the United States had limited success. During the first part of the twentieth century, the success of the labor movement was dependent on the state of the economy. When jobs were scarce such as during the depression following World War I and the Great Depression of the 1930s, unions had limited power. However, during World Wars I and II, when the supply of labor was low and the demand for labor was high. the unions were successful in improving the working conditions and wagess of their members.

From 1930 to the end of World War II, union membership grew dramatically. In 1930 there were 3.4 million union members or 7.5 percent of the workforce. By 1939, membership had increased by 159 percent to 8.8 million, (19.2 percent of the workforce). At the end of World War II, union membership grew by an additional 62.5 percent to 14.3 million, (27.1 percent of the workforce). As a percentage of the workforce, its number of members (17.0 million) peaked at 28.3 percent in 1954. In terms of an absolute number of members, the union rolls reached their zenith at 21.0 million which was 21.2 percent of the workforce in 1979. Since then union membership, both in absolute numbers and as a percent of the workforce, has been in a steady decline. By 2003, the number of union members had declined to 15.8 million, a mere 11.5 percent of those working.

Fig. 3-1 Graph of the number of employees belonging to a union in absolute numbers and as a percent of those employed from 1930–2003.
Source: *Calculated by Congressional Research Service from the monthly Current Population Survey*

The power of the union to gain benefits ebbed and flowed with the percentage of the workforce they controlled. In highly unionized industries such as the airlines, railroad, automobile, steel and supermarkets, they were able, by threatening to shut down individual companies or an entire industry, to elicit generous wage and benfit concession for its workers and retirees. However, since the 1980s, many United States industries have found themselves at a competitive disadvantage vis-à-vis foreign companies which had a much lower cost basis. By 2005, most of the American airlines had filed for bankruptcy protection, due in part to onerous union contracts they had entered into. The United States automobile industry found itself paying workers not to work and operating under union work rules, wages, and benefits that rendered them uncompetitive with their foreign counterparts. Unencumbered by the legacy costs of the US auto industry, foreign car companies have been able to produce cars in this country more profitably than General Motors, Ford and Chrysler. Many of those covered by union contracts have seen their wages and benefits reduced and their pensions drastically reduced or eliminated; others have lost their jobs and have been forced to seek employment elsewhere often at reduced pay and benefits.

The decline in union membership is not unique to the United States. From 1970-2000, among the twelve largest economies of the free world, 11 had experienced a decline in union membership as a percent of their workforces. The exception was Belgium which saw it increase by 32.1 percent. Of surprise is the fact that socialist France reduced its percentage of workers belonging to a union by 62.2 percent, an amount higher than any other country. Other countries saw reductions ranging from Italy's 6.2 percent reduction to Australia's 50.8 percent. The reduction in the United States was 45.5 percent. As the world's economies become more intertwined and the industrial capabilities of countries such as Brazil, India and China continue to progress, unions in the developed world will either have to accept lower wages and benefits for their members or continue to experience further declines in their membership rolls.

Relative Change in Union Membership as Percent of Workforce (1970–2000)	
FRANCE	-62.20%
AUSTRALIA	-50.80%
SWITZERLAND	-49.00%
UNITED STATES	-45.50%
JAPAN	-38.70%
NETHERLANDS	-36.70%
UNITED KINGDOM	-33.70%
GERMANY	-26.60%
SOUTH KOREA	-11.90%
CANADA	-11.10%
ITALY	-6.20%
BELGIUM	32.10%
Data: *Monthly Labor Review January 2006*	

Capitalism

Capitalism is best understood by comparing it to the two other major economic systems, Socialism and Communism. *The Columbia Encyclopedia*, Sixth Edition. 2001 defines these systems as follows:

- **Capitalism**—an economic system based on private ownership of the means of production, in which personal profit can be acquired through investment of capital and employment
- **Socialism** -a general term for the political and economic theory that advocates a system of collective or government ownership and management of the means of production
- **Communism**—fundamentally, a system of social organization in which property (especially real property and the means of production) is held in common

Capitalism, as distinct from Socialism and Communism, provides incentives for individuals to earn a profit from their investments. Joseph Schumpeter in his 1942 book, *Capitalism, Socialism, and Democracy*, coined the phrase "creative destruction" in which the current methodologies of doing things become obsolete or disadvantaged as a result of innovation. Innovation is the engine that provides long-term economic growth at the expense of the established companies interested in preserving the *status quo*.

An examination of the transformation that has occurred in the photographic industry provides a vivid illustration of Capitalism's creative destruction. For years Eastman Kodak dominated the market for inexpensive easy to use cameras, film, and developing pictures. Edwin Land's invention of the Polariod Instant Film Camera, first introduced to the public in 1948, allowed people to see their pictures within minutes without having to have their film developed. His invention captured that portion of the market that valued timeliness of seeing their pictures over the quality of their pictures. With the introduction in 1997 of the first megapixel digital cameras that didn't require the use of film, the photographic industry was radically transformed. These cameras captured The Polariod Corporation's market for "instant photography" and forced it into bankruptcy in 2001.

Eastman Kodak was forced to reinvent itself in the face of an accelerating decline in the use of film by consumers and professional photographers. Its once dominance of the market for film and film processing was destroyed. Instead of dominating the market for film and film processing, it has had to compete with camera manufacturers such as Nikon and Canon, consumer electronic companies such as Sony and Panasonic, as well as computer companies such as Hewlett-Packard and Dell. This was the second time that Kodak saw a market it once dominated relegated to innovation's scrap heap. The introduction of the camcorder in the 1980s eliminated the need to use film and have it developed and destroyed the home market for movie film. The impact on Eastman Kodak has been quite dramatic. Admitted to the Dow Jones Indutrial Average in 1930, it was removed in April 2004. Its stock price has fallen from a high of $67.41 in February 1997 to $24.85 by December 2005, a loss of 63.1 percent. As Eastman Kodak repositioned itself to more effectively compete in the electronic photography market, it has been forced to close facilities and realign its reduced workforce to deal with new technologies.

The photographic industry is not an isolated case. Consider the constant transformation of the retail industry. Starting with the general stores, catalog stores, department stores, five and dime stores, discount stores, big box reatilers, warehouse clubs, and internet merchants, the retail industry has embraced new ways of doing business at the expense of the *status quo*. Each change brought about winners, those that successfully embraced change, and losers, those that ignored the change or could not adapt to a new way of doing business. Some such as Kresge's successfully transformed itself from a five and dime store chain into a successful discount store chain known as K-Mart, which was an industry leader until Wal-Mart's success forced it into bankruptcy. Woolworth's, the original five and dime store also tried to reposition itself as a discount chain called Woolco, an edeavor that was not successful. Wal-Mart's success extends beyond the world of discounters to that of supermarkets. Its success in selling groceries has forced the incumbent supermarket operators to rethink their business models and to merge with each other in order to gain the critical mass necessary to compete against Wal-Mart.

Retailing is not the only industry that has undergone a series of metamorphoses. The automobile, airline, railroad, telephone, energy, financial services, computer, entertainment, and consumer electronics are also examples of industries that have had to take drastic actions to reposition themselves in the highly dynamic competitive environment in which they compete.

KEY TAKEAWAYS

1. **Success Does Not Just Happen.**

   In order to achieve success, one must determine his/her objectives, the criteria by which success will be measured, the steps necessary to achieve the desired objectives, and an implementation schedule along with measurable milestones. It is only by this rigid process of determining what you want to accomplish, defining how you are going to get there, and verifying that you are on the right track can you hope to be successful. While happenstance cannot be eliminated from the formula for success, you have to put yourself in a position to take advantage of it.

   If you want to be a doctor or lawyer, you must recognize that you will need to get an undergraduate as well as a graduate college degree and go through an apprentice program as a resident or a an associate. This means studying hard and forgoing many of life's diversions that your peers might be enjoying. If you are striving to be a professional athlete or musician, you must spend countless hours practicing and developing the necessary skills just to position yourself to be even considered for a chance to demonstrate your talents.

   Achieving a financial goal is no different than reaching a career goal. You must define your goal (how much you will need), how you are going to get there (how much you need to save per period of time, what will you invest in, what rate of return you expect to achieve, and how much risk are you willing to take), what are your interim milestones (what do your returns on your investment need to be by certain points in time) and when do you want to achieve your goal.

   Just as you just can't wish yourself to be a success in your chosen field of endeavor, you can't expect to magically have the money you want when you need it. You must develop the plan and have the perseverance to do what must be done.

2. **The Broader Your Foundation The More Opportunities There Are For You To Pursue.**

Whether it's our career or our investments, for most of us a broad base provides us with options to pursue and provides a modicum of protection against exogenous events. In most cases, a concentrated focus on one career path or specific investment, if all the planets are properly aligned, will provide greater success than a multifaceted approach. However, there is one highly significant *caveat*, and that is the odds of success are infinitesimally small. Just ask yourself how many of those little leaguers who dream of being a Derek Jeter, Alex Rodriguez, or Roger Clemens, will actually play in the minor leagues let alone be a superstar in the major league. The answer, damn few. Similarly, what is the probability of a single investment achieving all of your financial goals? Again, the answer is not encouraging.

We would be remiss if we ignored the danger of being so dispersed in our efforts that we do not have the necessary skills and background to take effective action to improve our careers or resources to improve our financial condition. Like the utility ballplayer, we want to position ourselves to be used at multiple positions. We do not want to be forced into a career path that ultimately leads us to a dead end. Even those that have chosen a profession, such as medicine or the law, that has a clearly defined career path, should ensure that even within their field of endeavor they have sufficient latitude to alter their area of specialization should circumstances warrant.

Investors should build their foundation with the proper mix of insurance and investments in equities and fixed income instruments. Insurance should be looked at as protection against unforeseen events such as destruction of property, health problems, disability, need for long term care, or death. At different times in our lives, our insurance needs change. So too it is with our investments. When our financial goals are further out in time, more risk can be taken. However, this should be done within the limits of prudence As our timeframe shortens, the prudent thing to do is to reallocate our investments to lower risk alternatives. Our investments, like our careers, must be managed. We should not diversify our investments to the point that each one is inconsequential to achieving our investment goals and our ability to manage them. Our goal is to be concentrated enough to be able to capitalize on the success of our investments. At the same time, we do not want any single investment's failure to jeopardize our financial health.

3. **Change Is An Inescapable Fact Of Life**

Just as the automobile destroyed the horse and buggy industry, so too will many of today's industries be irrevocably transformed by innovation. One of today's embryonic technologies may radically change an industry or set of industries much as the semiconductor affected the electronics and computer industries 50 years ago. Entire industries can and will become dominated by foreign, more efficient producers much as what happened to the United States consumer electronics companies. As this book is being written, countries such as India are becoming important factors in fields such as software development, engineering, call centers, etc. With the advent of high speed inexpensive communications, X-rays of a patient can be taken in New York and interpreted by a doctor in India; tax returns can be prepared anywhere in the world; and highly complex airplanes and semiconductors can be designed and manufactured by teams of companies throughout the world.

In our careers, we must continually keep abreast of changes that might affect our careers. Our area of specialty may be transformed by new technologies and/or methodologies that we must learn and adapt to or risk losing our jobs. Throughout our careers we must stay abreast of these changes and willingly adopt them. If the company that we work for continues to lose business, then it is inevitable that it will have to reduce costs and eliminate employees. One industry that historically has been infamous for this is the defense industry. The defense contractors assemble teams of highly skilled engineers and others to pursue a defense contract. Those companies that do not win the contract are forced to lay off many of those that they had hired. Under extreme conditions such as the winding down of the Cold War in the early 1990s, the entire defense industry was forced to contract. As a result, entire regions such as Southern California lost thousands of jobs.

When an entire geographical area loses jobs, those affected must condition themselves to the need to accept positions in other parts of the country, in other industries, in other specialties, and often at lower pay. Sometimes, we can see the storm approaching and start to position ourselves to start seeking new job opportunities. Other times, it may come when we least expect it. Regardless, accept the reality of the situation and start doing something about it. You may feel the need to complain and feel sorry for yourself but that won't solve your quandary. At such a time, get over your emotional needs and reexamine your career plan and adapt it to the new realities. The sooner you develop a plan of action the sooner you can proceed to the next phase of your life. In many cases, with careful planning and a whole lot of blood, sweat and tears you may actually be able to advance your career development.

As with our careers, our investments can be affected by change. As new technologies emerge, the dynamics of entire industries can change and transform industry leaders into followers or inconsequential participants in the industry. Consider the photographic industry discussed earlier in this book, the steel industry which has been transformed both by technology and lower cost foreign competitors, and the automobile industry that once dominated the US economy being forced to fight for its survival in the face of intense foreign competition. Investors in these and other companies have suffered significant reduction in the value of their investments.

We must keep up with changes in the industries in which we invest and understand the potential implications on the companies in which we have invested. If we believe that change will negatively affect the strategic position of a company in which we have a stake, then we should consider reducing or eliminating our exposure to the company. If the change will have only a transitory effect on the company and not diminish its long term outlook, then we should hold on to our position in that company or even increase it. While in theory we could sell our stock to protect our profits and buy it back at a lower price before its prospects improve, the reality is that this is extremely difficult for the non-professional investor. Similarly, companies in which we do not have a position that encounter what we deem to be temporary setbacks should be examined as a potential candidate for investment while its stock price is depressed and before its improved prospects have been factored into its price.

4.   Don't Entrust Your Success To Others

Quite often when faced with a critical decision, we seek the counsel of others. Getting various perspectives regarding how to proceed can be very helpful. However, often when the decision is the most difficult, we can quite easily fall into the trap of believing that those from whom we have sought counsel know more than we and therefore their advice must be right. It behooves us to fully understand the recommendation and all of its ramifications to us both favorable and unfavorable.

In the early stages of our Childhood Stage, we must rely on our parents and other authority figures to make the right decisions for us. But by the time we have completed our Adolescence Phase, we should have a sense of potential career paths that we might want to pursue. Unless, we choose a path that is consistent with our abilities and interests, it is exceedingly difficult to achieve success despite whatever sacrifices we make. A father that wants his son or daughter to follow in his footsteps does him/her a disservice if the child wants to take his/her life in a different direction. Most people can accept the notion of not letting someone force them into a career that is not consistent with their interests.

It is when we are faced with a decision regarding something that we are not knowledgeable, that we should rely on experts. For example, when we have an unusual pain, we go to the doctor. The doctor will examine us and may perform specialized tests (blood tests, x-rays, CT scans, etc,) to determine the cause of our problem. If these tests do not reveal anything, then we feel relieved. The thought as to whether our doctor performed the appropriate tests for our complaint never enters our mind. We put our trust in our physician. Since the knowledge of medicine for most of us is quite limited we have no choice. On the other hand, if the tests reveal a problem, our doctor will discuss his diagnosis and his recommended course of action. If the cure is relatively simple such as taking some pills for a few days, we willingly follow the doctor's direction. If the diagnosis is more complicated and requires surgery, chemotherapy, or radiation, we would discuss the doctor's recommended course of action with him. In many cases, we would seek a second opinion from another physician. It would be impossible for us, even if we were a physician ourselves, to perform a complex procedure such as surgery on ourselves. In situations such as this, we have no choice but to entrust our lives to an expert.

When it comes to financial matters, many of us are not comfortable making decisions by ourselves. We seek the advice of our relatives, friends, business associates, and in some cases a financial advisor. We rationalize this behavior by thinking to ourselves that they surely must know more than we do. In some cases, this may in fact, be true. However, we, not our sources of advice, will either enjoy or suffer the consequences of the decision. If, based on their advice, we make money, we feel good. On the other hand, if, based on their advice, we lose money, we feel not so good.

Typically our acquaintances will tell us about an investment they have made and how well they did. They boast of the profits they have made and conveniently forget to mention any of their losses. The naïve among us, wanting to share in their success, would make the same investment. The problem with this style of investing in our friends' winners is that most of the money from that investment may have already been made. Let us assume that our friend tells us about his investment in the XYZ company for which he paid $10.00 per share and after six months trades at $25.00 per share, an historic high. We, wanting to believe that we too can profit from this investment, contemplate purchasing stock in XYZ at $25.00. The question we must answer for ourselves is whether a stock that has increased in value 150 percent in 6 months has the potential to further increase in price? If we buy the stock and it falls to $20.00 per share, we have lost twenty percent of our investment; meanwhile our friend is making $10.00 per share or a 100 percent profit.

Many of us are constantly bombarded with investment opportunities that promise returns that are seemingly very attractive. As a general rule, if the recommendations are from an unknown source, ignore them. **DO NOT UNDER ANY CIRCUMSTANCES INVEST IN SOMETHING OFFERING RETURNS THAT ARE TOO GOOD TO BE TRUE.** These people can be quite persuasive and persistent. They are interested in supporting their families. They are not as interested in helping you achieve your financial objectives.

A good financial adviser can be an invaluable resource in helping to formulate a strategy for achieving your financial objectives. He/she can help you understand the investment options that are most appropriate for you and help you in developing your plan for achieving your objectives. After your plan has been completed, it is up to you to implement it. Most people should be able to proceed from this point on their own.

5.   **The Later You Get Started The Harder It Will Be to Succeed**

It would be nice if we knew what career path we wanted to pursue by the time we reached our sophomore year of high school. If we did, we would know what courses to take and if we wanted to pursue a college education, then we would be able to select colleges whose curriculum was consistent with our career objectives. Unfortunately, many of us do not have any idea of what we want to do with our future at this point in our lives. This may occur for many reasons whose explanation is beyond the scope of this book. By the time of graduation from high school, many still do not have career objectives and either get a job while they try to determine what they want to do with their lives or pursue a college education in order to obtain a well rounded education. Others in their junior or senior years decide that they want to go to college without having the necessary prerequisites and have to delay their applications while they take the courses at a community college or similar institution to satisfy the admission requirements of the colleges in which they are interested. In this case, they would have added one to two years to the time required to complete their college education.

While not having chosen a career path while in high school is not good, graduating from college with a bachelor's degree and no potential career goals is even worse. At this juncture of their lives, those without career goals often take a job for the sake of having an income, take time off to tour Europe, or pursue an advanced degree in order to avoid deciding what career path they wish to pursue. At some point in time in their lives, our lost souls will have an epiphany and select their career path. At this point, their education may be consistent with their chosen profession. Or, as it happens more often than one would expect, they discover that they need additional education and must spend one to six or more years of study in order to position themselves to pursue their career interests. In extreme cases, they may find their life's progression at the Adolescence Stage of their lives based on their maturation process while chronologically they are at Phase I of the Young Adulthood Stage.

Many of us will face a mid-life crisis, where we critically analyze our lives and, in some cases, decide that we would like to pursue a different career path. Our new career direction can, in extreme cases, require years of additional education and having to start at an entry point in that new career path as in the case of a nurse who decides that he/she wants to become a doctor and must go to medical school for four years and intern at a hospital for three more years. Or consider, the fifty year old engineer who has not kept pace with the skill sets needed to perform his/her specialty and must learn new skills at a time in his/her life where he/she must provide for his/her family's need for food, clothing, shelter and often college, as well as saving for his/her approaching retirement. Upon developing a new set of skills, his/her age puts him/her at a disadvantage in the job market for an entry level position as compared to someone who is twenty of more years his/her junior.

With respect to investing for long term purposes, the longer you have to invest the more realistic it is to achieve your objective. As discussed under Retirement Strategies, if one invests his/her savings over a forty year period it is much easier to provide for one's retirement years than if one has only thirty, twenty or ten years.

At the risk of being redundant, it is important for the reader to understand the deleterious effects of procrastinating in determining his/her career path and starting an investment program.

6.   Hubris Can Be Fatal

Being confident in one's abilities can be an admirable trait. When as a young child we have a problem, we believe that no matter what it is that bothers us, our parents can make everything right. As we get older we acquire a set of skills in which we are confident and recognize our limitations. Some of us develop a feeling of invincibility and believe that there is nothing in which we cannot excel. Inevitably, these people will receive their comeuppance. In school, believing that they know everything, they do not study for an exam and as a result receive a poor grade. As an athlete or an entertainer not appreciating the need to practice, they embarrass themselves at a critical moment. In our careers, believing that they are omniscient, they fail to consider the points of view of others. As a result, they pursue a course of action that adversely affect their own careers as well as the careers or, at the extreme, the lives of others. Consider the case of the airline pilot who tries to fly a plane while under the influence of alcohol, the doctor who treats a patient rather than referring him/her to a specialist, or the CEO who fraudulently inflates his/her company's performance or diverts funds in order to fatten his/her wallet. In recent years there have been far too many examples of executives who have put their own personal interests ahead of their employees and stockholders.

Some of us may be fortunate to achieve extraordinary success in our careers or investments. We come to believe that we are infallible and our past success will be the norm rather than a fortuitous aberration. We come to believe that we will always succeed and like the inveterate gambler, place our careers or our wealth on the line and roll the dice with our careers and finances. Such folks will inevitably come up snake eyes. Even the most successful investors are not immune to snatching losses from the jaws of profits

We should understand what reasonable expectations for our careers and investments are. We should not fool ourselves and believe that we can do no wrong with our careers and our investments. Just because we got a hole-in-one on the first hole of today's round of golf, only the most arrogant among us would expect to achieve such a feat all the time. Amazingly, there are many among us who behave this way by the manner in which they pursue their careers or select their investments

7. **That Light At The End Of Your Career Can Either Be A Freight Train Or The Dawning Of A Brand New Life**

Unless you were fortunate enough to have been born into wealth, your career and the financial resources that you will need throughout your life rests squarely on your shoulders. Whether you developed a rigorous and broad academic background, pursued a carefully thought-out career path, and skillfully managed your finances will probably become apparent to you only when you reach the Old Age Stage of your life. Then you will be able to evaluate your career path and the tradeoffs you made between career and family as well as between consumption and saving.

It is at this time that you will know whether that light at the end of the proverbial tunnel is the dawn of a brand new life or a freight train barreling down on you with box cars loaded with problems. Unfortunately, if you did not start preparing for this stage of your life, it is too late to rectify your situation. You can't blame your parents, teachers, bosses, families, friends, financial advisors or anyone but yourself. The most you can expect is empathy for your predicament. Your success is something that cannot be delegated to others. A lifetime of frivolity and irresponsibility cannot be rectified in the twilight of your existence.

8. **Success Brings Its Own Set Of Issues To Be Confronted**

As we progress in our careers from a neophyte who is eager to grow professionally to a more seasoned individual, the expectations that others set for us change. Our performance is measured at ever higher levels of expectations. In addition, others expect us to support them in achieving their career expectations. Not only are we evaluated by our superiors but also by our peers as well as our subordinates. What was acceptable performance yesterday may become unacceptable today and certainly tomorrow.

As we achieve financial success, many of us become what is referred to as "Qualified Investors." This will expose us to those seeking our participation in oil & gas partnerships, leasing deals, motion pictures, condominium conversions, etc. Those exposed to such investment opportunities should ask themselves why they should invest in such endeavors and how does such an investment support their financial strategy and objectives that they have established for themselves.

In addition to these challenges, our friends, the number of which tends to grow exponentially with our success, expect us to treat them when dining out and sometimes even lend them money. Just because you become a success does not mean that you are obligated to transfer the fruits of your success to others. Rather, you should do it, if and only if, it is something that you want to do not something that others unreasonably expect of you.

9.   **Continue to Reinvest in Yourself**

Perhaps the most important concept to take away from this section is the need for reinvestment in our careers and our portfolios. Just because we may have completed our formal education, it does not mean that we are through learning. Learning is a life long process. By acquiring new or extended knowledge/skills we should be able to adapt to the ever accelerating pace on innovation. If our own individual skills do not measure up to the requirements or our chosen filed of endeavor, then our careers and our ability to earn a living will become endangered.

As with our careers, we should reinvest in our investment portfolios. Rather than spend the interest or dividends that we receive from our investments, we should take those proceeds and reinvest them. The returns generated from reinvestment can be substantial over the ten, twenty, thirty or forty years that we build our retirement wealth.

SECTION II

PLANNING CONSIDERATIONS

Before a retirement strategy can be developed there are certain factors that need to be considered. They are:
- Inflation
- Available investments

Inflation

Simply stated, inflation is the decline in the amount of goods and services that can be purchased with a fixed sum of money. The impact on those investing for their retirement is that it will cost more to purchase things in the future. Consequently they need to factor in these increased costs when determining how much money they will need to support themselves in their retirement years.

Those born in 1940 and retiring at age sixty five in 2005 would have seen inflation average 4.2 percent over their lifetime. Based on the actual annual rates of inflation, those persons upon reaching retirement age would have found that it would take $17.14 to purchase what $1.00 purchased in 1940 when they were born.

Currently, inflationary forces in the United States are relatively subdued. However, from 1973 to 1981 prices increased by 83.3 percent. During that time period, many retirees were forced to dramatically adjust their standard of living to accommodate the reduced purchasing power of their income stream.

Despite periods of inflation and deflation, the United States has averaged a 3.26 percent annual increase in the price of goods and services from 1928–2005.

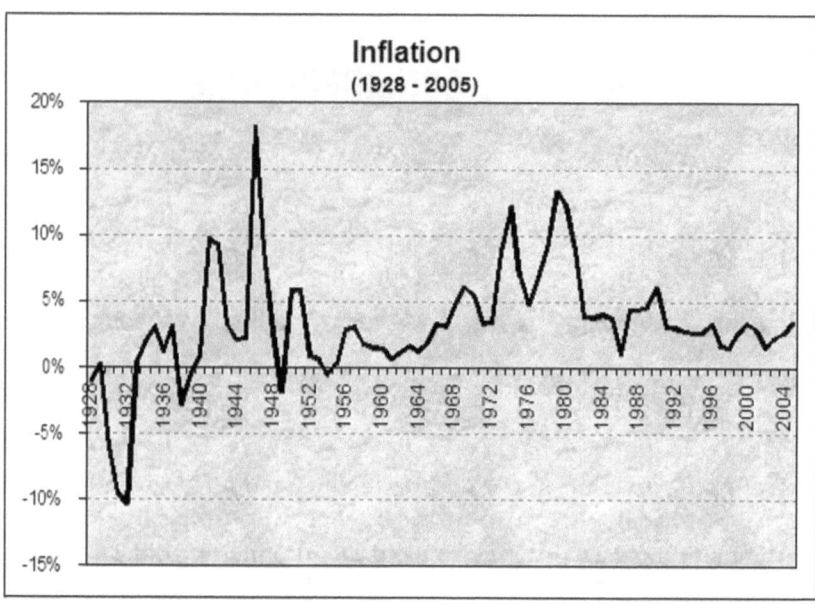

Fig. 5-1 Annual rates of inflation in United States from 1928–2005
Data: *Bureau of Labor Statistics*

With the exception of the Great Depression years of 1928 to 1932, when the purchasing power of the dollar increased, the purchasing power of the 1928 dollar has been steadily decreasing. A dollar in 2005 purchased only 6.9 percent of what it did in 1928 based on the actual annual rates of inflation during that time span

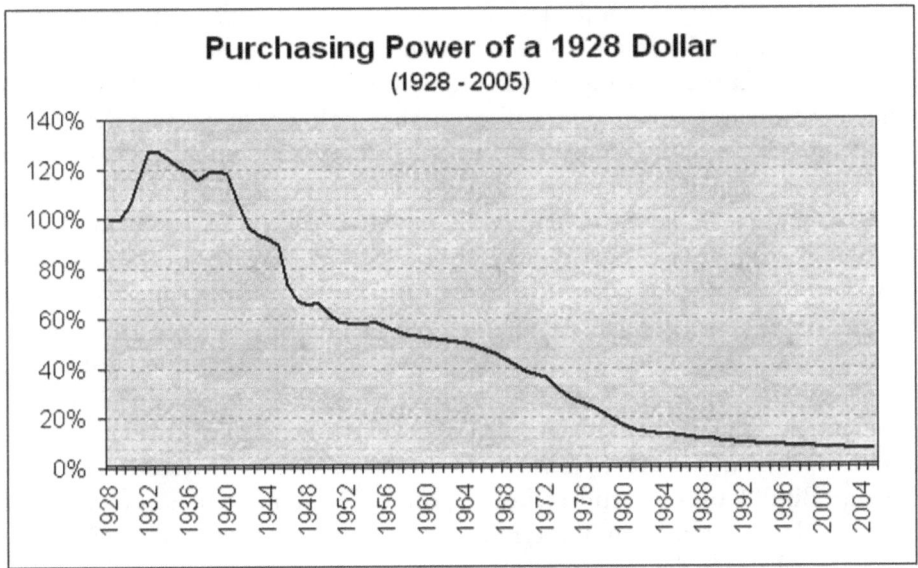

Fig. 5-2 Purchasing power of a 1928 dollar based on the annual rates of inflation from 1928–2005

Data: *Bureau of Labor Statistics*

Inflation is important because it affects the investment opportunities available to investors. Fixed income investments, in general, expose the investor to loss of purchasing power at maturity. (Inflation indexed Treasuries protect investors from inflation by adjusting the principal paid at maturity by the rate of inflation). Equities, in theory, can compensate investors with price appreciation and potential increases in dividend payouts. However, equities may, in fact, suffer as a result of inflation. This is especially true when inflation is accompanied by little or no growth, stagflation

Available Investments

Before the various types of available investments can be discussed, it is important to define what constitutes investors and to differentiate them from speculators.

- **Investors** are those who prudently commit their capital in order to gain a financial return
- **Speculators** trade in financial instruments that have an above average risk in return for an expectation of above average returns

Investors carefully weigh the relationship between potential risks and rewards and commit their funds only where it is advantageous to do so. They do not invest more than they can afford to lose and never risk their entire net worth on a single investment. Over time they diversify their holdings by putting their assets in different classes of investments. When one first starts investing and has limited funds, it is not possible to put money economically in more than one investment class. For those making investments with limited resources, their emphasis should be on limiting their risk. They should forego potentially greater profits in favor of preserving their capital. These initial investments should be liquid and available to be deployed in times of financial need.

As shown in Fig. 5-3 below, Treasury Bills (T-Bills), which are backed by the full faith and credit of the United States have the lowest risk and thus have correspondingly lower returns than more risky investments such as small capitalization stocks. As one moves from short term fixed income investments such as Treasury Bills (T-Bills), Certificates of Deposit (CDs) to intermediate term 5 Year Treasury Notes to long term Government Bonds with maturities of 10–30 years, the principal risk is that of inflation's eroding the purchasing power of the principal and not of the issuer defaulting on its obligations. In the case of equity investments, the risk is one of suffering substantial loss of the amount invested or even the entire investment should the company that issued the common stock file for bankruptcy. As one moves from the S&P 500 Large Capitalization Stocks to smaller capitalization stocks, this risk increases. Smaller companies generally have less access to funds to tide them over in times of adversity than larger ones.

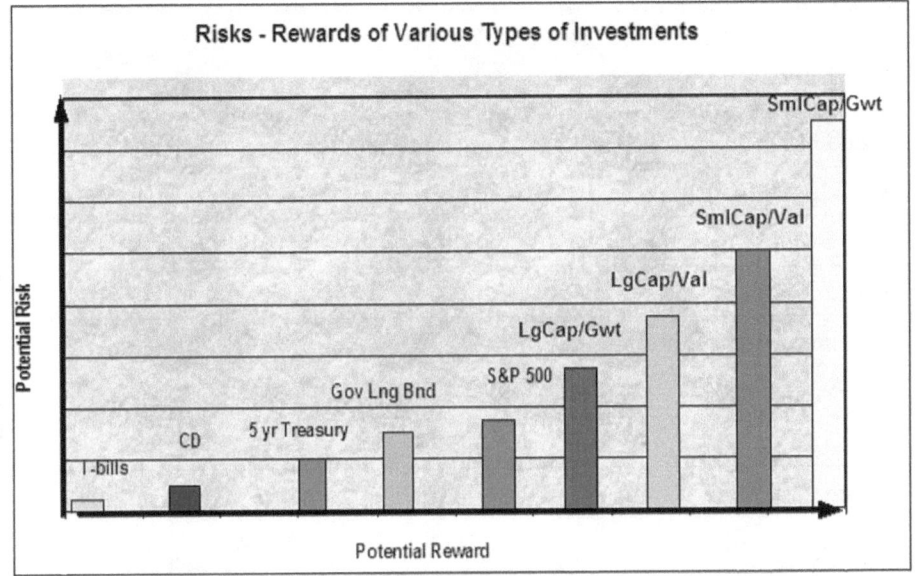

Fig. 5-3 Chart showing the relationship between Potential Risk and Potential Reward of various investment classes

An analysis of the rates of returns available to investors from 1928–2005 reveals a wide range of possible returns.

This time period was chosen because it includes the Great Depression, economic expansions, recessions, inflation, deflation, stagflation, natural disasters, supply disruptions, wars, peace and terrorism. There is no reason to believe that investors should not expect similar conditions to occur over their lifetime along with the commensurate returns and risks to their investments.

For example, 6 month Treasury Bills, one of the lowest risk investments yielded an average of 3.83 percent. During this timeframe, the actual returns ranged from a minimum return of 0.00 percent to a maximum return of 14.70 percent. Small Capitalization Growth Stocks, a riskier investment than Treasury Bills, returned an average of 13.80 percent with a minimum return of-46.30 percent and a maximum of 158.10 percent. While, as they say on Wall Street, past returns are not indicative of future returns, one should carefully take into consideration historical returns when analyzing potential investments.

HISTORICAL RATES OF RETURN (1928—2005)			
INVESTMENT TYPE	**Annual Rate of Return**		
INCOME	Minimum	Average	Maximum
Treasury Bills	0.00%	3.83%	14.70%
Five Year Treasury Notes	-5.10%	5.35%	29.10%
Government Long Bond	-9.20%	5.66%	40.40%
EQUITIES			
Standard & Poor's 500	-43.40%	11.98%	54.00%
Large Capitalization Value	-58.70%	15.11%	115.50%
Large Capitalization Growth	-35.80%	11.08%	50.20%
Small Capitalization Growth	-46.30%	13.80%	158.10%
Small Capitalization Value	-52.20%	18.53%	118.10%
Data: *www.gummy-stuff.org*			

In the Journey Called Life chapter of this book, the importance of starting early for retirement was stated as being essential in creating a source of wealth that can be used later in life. The later one starts to accumulate wealth, the more aggressive one has to be in investing his/her capital. Aggressive investment opportunities also have commensurate risks of loss of principal.

RETIREMENT STRATEGIES

To restate the obvious, disciplined investors develop and execute their own individual investment strategy whose objectives are to accumulate sufficient financial assets beginning in the Adolescence Phase of their Childhood through Young Adulthood and into Middle Age that will support the needs of their growing family and to provide for themselves during their Old Age. They strike that balance between consumption and saving for retirement that allows them to live the lifestyle they have chosen and to provide for their futures. Upon retirement, the emphasis changes from managing the accumulation of wealth to managing the withdrawal of funds to support their retirement needs. They must switch their asset allocations from emphasizing wealth creation to income generation and inflation protection. In addition, they must define their retirement lifestyle and determine the amount of money it will take to support it, how much of that money will come from their pensions, Social Security benefits, dividends and interest income, and withdrawal of principal from their portfolios.

When developing any investment strategy, it is important to remember that there are three variables that will determine the success or failure of that strategy. They are the amount of the investment, the time horizon of the investment and the rate of return that will occur over the life of the investment. Of these three variables, there are two that are completely under the control of the investor. They are the amount and time horizon of the investment. The actual annual rates of return that the investment portfolio will generate are not under the control of the investor. However, the longer the time horizon is, the higher the probability of achieving adequate returns.

In The Journey Called Life chapter of this book, three retirement strategies (the optimal, possible and improbable) were discussed. The rest of this chapter addresses some guidelines to consider in implementing each of these strategies.

Optimal Retirement Strategy

The optimal strategy is one in which there is sufficient time to reasonably expect to achieve a defined set of objectives. It consists of four distinct phases that correlate with the stages and phases of Life's Progression.

Under this strategy an individual develops a disciplined savings program that allocates 6 percent of his/her annual salary to first creating a safety net that can be used in times of financial need and then to a retirement saving program. In each phase and sub-phase of this strategy, allocations between saving for a safety net and retirement change as the safety net goals of each phase are reached. An integral part of this strategy is saving 6 percent of annual salary to provide a safety net and a retirement fund.

This strategy assumes the following:

- the annual salary will increase at the rate of inflation
- the safety net goal for each phase and sub-phase must be highly liquid in order to be able to be a source of funds to meet unforeseen financial needs
- any interest income earned on the liquid portion of the safety net will compensate for any loss of purchasing power as a result of inflation
- once the safety net goal of a sub-phase has been met, the amount saved will be allocated between increasing the safety net and saving for retirement
- any excess safety net contributions will be invested in Certificates of Deposit that will earn 6.68 percent per year, the average yield on CDs from 1964-2005
- retirement contributions invested in an S&P 500 Index Mutual Fund or Exchange Traded Fund will earn 12.0 percent, the average return from 1928 to 2005; those invested in CDs will earn 6.68 percent
- if actual rates of return from investments are lower than assumed in this strategy, the amount invested will be increased to compensate for the lower returns
- at retirement, 4 percent of the amount saved will be withdrawn annually. This means that at retirement twenty five times the annual salary at age sixty five must have been accumulated in order to safely withdraw 4 percent annually to maintain the standard of living enjoyed before retirement and to reduce the probability of outliving ones savings.

Phase I

Phase I of the Optimal Retirement Strategy corresponds to the Adolescence Phase of the Childhood Stage of Life's Progressions and covers ages twenty one to twenty seven. Starting at age twenty one and continuing to age twenty four, 6 percent of annual salary is placed in a savings or money market checking account. At age twenty five, the phase goal of having a safety net of three months will have been reached. The adequacy of this and the other safety net requirements are ultra conservative. From twenty five to twenty seven, the safety net savings contribution is reduced to 1 percent of annual salary and the remaining 5 percent is placed in an S&P 500 Index Mutual Fund or Exchange Traded Fund. From ages twenty six to twenty seven, the safety net contributions are placed in Certificates of Deposit.

At the end of Phase I which corresponds to twenty seven years of age, 108.8 percent of the safety net goal and 0.8 percent of the retirement goal will have been reached.

PHASE I SAVINGS ACTIONS			
Age	• **Build a financial safety net of three months salary** • **Start saving for retirement fund of twenty five times annual income.**	**Percent of Goal**	
		Safety Net	**Retirement**
Adolescence Phase of Childhood Stage of Life's Progressions			
21	• Set aside 6 percent of income into liquid assets such as a savings account or money market checking account each year	24.0%	0.0%
22	• Continue saving 6 percent of income annually	48.0%	0.0%
23		72.0%	0.0%
24		96.0%	0.0%
25	• Reduce saving for safety net to 1 percent • Save 5 percent of annual income for retirement in S&P 500 Index Fund or ETF.	100.0%	0.2%
26	• Invest the 1 percent safety net contribution in a CD	104.3%	0.5%
27	• Continue saving 5 percent for retirement	108.8%	0.8%

Phase II

Phase II of this strategy is divided into three sub-phases that correspond to the three phases of the Young Adulthood Stage of Life's Progressions. Phase II-A covers ages twenty eight to thirty four, Phase II-B ages thirty five to forty one, and Phase II-A ages forty two to forty eight.

Phase II-A

In Phase II-A, the safety net requirements are increased from three to four months annual salary. The reason for the increase is that as one becomes older his/her financial obligations tend to increase. Furthermore, it often becomes harder to find employment in the event of a layoff. From twenty eight to thirty three, 1 percent of annual salary is placed in a savings account or money market checking account for the safety net and 5 percent is invested in S&P 500 Index Funds or ETF's for retirement. At age thirty four, the safety net savings are placed in a CD while the retirement funds continue to be invested in the S&P 500.

At the end of Phase II-A, 106.6 percent of the safety net goal (4.26 months salary) and 3.9 percent of the retirement goal will have been reached.

PHASE II-A SAVINGS ACTIONS			
Age	• Increase financial safety net to four months salary • Continue saving for retirement fund of twenty five times annual income.	Percent of Goal	
		Safety Net	Retirement
Phase I of Young Adulthood Stage of Life's Progressions			
28	• Invest 1 percent of annual salary for safety net in a savings account or money market checking account each year. • Do not touch safety net funds previously invested in CDs. • Continue saving 5 percent of annual income for retirement in S&P 500 Index Fund or ETF.	85.1%	1.1%
29		88.5%	1.4%
30		92.0%	1.8%
31		95.6%	2.3%
32		99.1%	2.8%
33		102.7%	3.3%
34	• Invest the 1 percent safety net contribution in a CD • Continue saving 5 percent for retirement	106.6%	3.9%

Phase II-B

In Phase II-B, the safety net is increased from four to five months salary. From ages thirty five to thirty nine, 1 percent of the annual salary is placed in a savings account or money market checking account. As in Phase II-A, 5 percent of the annual salary is invested in the S&P 500. With the saving net goal for this subphase reached, 1 percent of annual salary will be shifted to CDs while 5 percent is allocated to retirement savings from ages forty to forty one.

The end of Phase II-B sees the safety net at 108.8 percent of its goal or 5.4 months and the retirement funds at 10.9 percent of its goal.

PHASE II-B SAVINGS ACTIONS			
Age	• Increase financial safety net to five months salary • Continue saving for retirement fund of twenty five times annual income.	Percent of Goal	
		Safety Net	Retirement
Phase II of Young Adulthood Stage of Life's Progressions			
35	• Invest 1 percent of annual salary for safety net in a savings account or money market checking account each year. • Do not touch safety net funds previously invested in CDs. • Continue saving 5 percent of annual income for retirement in S&P 500 Index Fund or ETF.	88.4%	4.6%
36		91.6%	5.4%
37		94.8%	6.3%
38		98.1%	7.3%
39		101.4%	8.4%
40	• Invest the 1 percent safety net contribution in a CD • Continue saving 5 percent for retirement	105.0%	9.6%
41		108.8%	10.9%

Phase II-C

The safety net is increased from five to six months in Phase II-C. From ages forty two to forty four, 1 percent of annual income is placed in the same liquid investments used previously to increase the safety net and 5 percent is invested in the S&P 500 for retirement. From ages forty five to forty eight, the 1 percent safety net contributions is placed in CDs while the 5 percent retirement contributions continue to be placed in the S&P 500.

The end of Phase II finds the safety net at seven months or 116.8 percent of the Phase II-C goal and the retirement fund at 26.5 percent of its goal.

PHASE II-C SAVINGS ACTIONS			
Age	• **Increase financial safety net to six months salary** • **Continue saving for retirement fund of twenty five times annual income.**	**Percent of Goal**	
		Safety Net	**Retirement**
Phase III of Young Adulthood Stage of Life's Progressions			
42	• Invest 1 percent of annual salary for safety net in a savings account or money market checking account each year. • Do not touch safety net funds previously invested in CDs. • Continue saving 5 percent of annual income for retirement in S&P 500 Index Fund or ETF.	93.9%	12.5%
43		97.2%	14.2%
44		100.7%	16.1%
45	• Invest the 1 percent safety net contribution in a CD • Continue saving 5 percent for retirement	104.3%	18.3%
46		108.2%	20.7%
47		112.4%	23.4%
48		116.8%	26.5%

Phase III

Phase III of this strategy is divided into three sub-phases that correspond to the three phases of the Middle Age Stage of Life's Progressions. By the time one reaches forty eight, the 1 percent that had been saved to provide an ever increasing safety net can be added to the 5 percent being saved for retirement. The reason for this is that the annual interest earned on the Certificates of Deposit should provide the additional safety net goals of each of the three sub-phases of Phase III. If the prevailing returns on CDs are lower, the allocation of investment funds will need to be adjusted accordingly.

Phase III-A

Starting with Phase III-A, all retirement savings contributions will be invested in Certificates of Deposit from age forty nine until retirement. This will provide a liquid source of income to fund retirement needs.

By the time one has reached the end of Phase III-A, his/her safety net will be 8.33 months salary or 119.1 percent of this sub-phase's goal of 7 months and 60.7 percent of the retirement goal.

PHASE III-A SAVINGS ACTIONS			
Age	• Increase financial safety net to seven months salary • Continue saving for retirement fund of twenty five times annual income.	Percent of Goal	
		Safety Net	Retirement
Phase I of Middle Age Stage of Life's Progressions			
49	• Continue to not touch safety net funds previously invested in CDs. • Save 6 percent of annual income for retirement. • Invest retirement savings in CDs.	102.3%	29.9%
50		104.7%	33.7%
51		107.2%	38.0%
52		109.9%	42.8%
53		112.8%	48.4%
54		115.9%	54.1%
55		119.1%	60.7%

Phase III-B

As in Phase III-A, the 6 percent of annual salary allocated for retirement is invested in CDs. During Phase III-B, the amount invested for retirement will have reached 100 percent of the retirement goal of twenty five times annual earnings. Interest from the safety net CDs will provide enough to increase the safety net to 10.4 months or 130.4 percent of the 8 month goal. The retirement funds will be at 135.0 percent of its goal. Since the retirement savings goal would have been met at age sixty, one could decide to retire early.

	PHASE III-B SAVINGS ACTIONS			
Age	• Increase financial safety net to eight months salary • Continue saving for retirement fund of twenty five times annual income.	Percent of Goal		
		Safety Net	Retirement	
Phase II of Middle Age Stage of Life's Progressions				
56	• Continue to not touch safety net funds previously invested in CDs. • Continue saving 6 percent of annual income for retirement. • Invest retirement savings in CDs.	107.3%	68.1%	
57		110.6%	76.4%	
58		114.0%	85.7%	
59		117.7%	96.0%	
60		121.7%	107.6%	
61		125.9%	120.5%	
62		130.4%	135.0%	

Phase III-C

Phase III-C continues the investment actions of Phase III-B. 6 percent of income continues to be invested in CDs for retirement. The CDs previously allocated for the safety net will provide enough income to increase the safety net to 11.7 months or 129.6 percent of the nine month goal. Savings for retirement will be at 189.4 percent of the goal of twenty five times annual salary.

	PHASE III-C SAVINGS ACTIONS		
	• **Increase financial safety net to nine months salary**	**Percent of Goal**	
Age	• **Continue saving for retirement fund of twenty five times annual income.**	**Safety Net**	**Retirement**
	Phase III of Middle Age Stage of Life's Progressions		
63	• Continue to not touch safety net funds previously invested in CDs.	120.2%	151.1%
64		124.8%	169.2%
65	• Continue saving 6 percent of annual income for retirement in CDs.	129.6%	189.4%

At the conclusion of Phase III of the Optimal Retirement Strategy, the funds saved for a safety net can be used as source of income during retirement. If one had followed the guidelines for this strategy and the assumptions regarding the average rates of return that could be achieved turned out to be valid, one would have accumulated 48.3 times his/her annual salary. If interest rates of CDs averaged only 5 percent per year and the S&P 500 returned only 10 percent per year, all other factors being equal, then one would have twenty seven times his/her annual salary upon which to retire.

Phase IV

Phase IV is the transition from saving for retirement to actual retirement. If the guidelines of the Optimal Retirement Strategy had been followed and its underlying assumptions were reasonably accurate, then retirement can be a time to enjoy life without worrying about money. During retirement, investments in Certificates of Deposit and the S&P 500 Index would continue to earn the same rates of return as they did prior to retirement. The recommended approach for withdrawing funds for living expenses consists of the following steps:

- Upon retirement at age sixty five:
  - Transfer 7.3 months salary from the S&P 500 Index fund into a money market account. If the balance of the liquid asset portion of the safety net was placed in a savings account, then transfer that money into a money

market checking account as needed. This will provide twelve months of living expenses.

- Transfer 102 months salary from the S&P 500 Index funds to Certificates of Deposit or Treasuries. The maturities should be laddered so that every month, one month's salary will mature and be ready for use if the liquid assets are not adequate to cover expenses. Together with the retirement funds that had been set aside for retirement previously this pool of money will represent ten years living expenses. While this may seem excessively conservative, it is at this stage of one's life that one needs protection from the vicissitudes of the stock market. It is up to the individual to determine how much risk he/she is willing to assume.

- Every year thereafter transfer twelve months salary, adjusted for inflation, from the S&P 500 Index funds to the money market checking account for living expenses.

Under this retirement strategy, would one not have to reduce his/her standard of living or outlive his/her money. In fact, the funds would continue to grow because the rate of return on these funds would exceed the rate of withdrawal from these funds.

OPTIMAL RETIREMENT STRATEGY CASH FLOW									
	Money Market Checking Account				Certificates of Deposit			S&P 500 Index Fund		
Age	Transfers	Withdrawals	Interest	Balance	Net Transfers	Interest	Balance	Transfers	Return	Balance
65				4.7			30.0			545.2
70	55.3	-60.0	NM	0.0	102.0	50.4	182.4	-157.3	316.0	703.9
75	60.0	-60.0	NM	0.0	0.0	69.6	252.0	-60.0	511.2	1,155.1
80	60.0	-60.0	NM	0.0	0.0	96.2	348.2	-60.0	855.2	1,950.4
85	60.0	-60.0	NM	0.0	0.0	132.9	481.1	-60.0	1,461.5	3,351.9
90	60.0	-60.0	NM	0.0	0.0	183.6	664.8	-60.0	2,529.9	5,821.7
95	60.0	-60.0	NM	0.0	0.0	253.7	918.5	-60.0	4,412.8	10,174.5
100	60.0	-60.0	NM	0.0	0.0	350.6	1,269.1	-60.0	7,731.1	17,845.6

Under this strategy, one would have enough retirement funds to live past one hundred and still have 160 months of salary in the unlikely case that during retirement one was not able to achieve a positive return on his/her retirement portfolio.

Those who sacrificed to implement these guidelines and achieved the assumed rates of return on their investments would be able to enjoy a retirement free from financial worries.

Possible Retirement Strategy

The Possible Retirement Strategy can achieve the retirement fund objective of having twenty five times annual salary upon retirement. Unlike the Optimal Retirement Strategy, there is no margin of safety in this strategy.

The factor that differentiates the Possible Retirement Strategy from the Optimal Retirement Strategy is the time available to save for retirement. Under the Optimal Retirement Strategy one has from age twenty five to sixty five to save for retirement; the Possible Retirement Strategy one has only from ages thirty five to sixty five, a difference of ten years. There are only two factors that can be prudently adjusted to compensate for the loss of those years. These factors are the amount of money to be saved each year and how those funds are to be allocated between building a safety net and building a retirement fund.

There are two risks inherent in this strategy. One is that a safety net of three months annual salary may not suffice. The other is that the annual returns from investing in the S&P 500 may be less than 10.0 percent

The Possible Retirement Strategy consists of three phases that correlate with the stages and phases of Life's Progressions. Under this strategy, one saves 10 percent of his/her annual salary to be divided between establishing a safety net and building a retirement fund. This strategy is based on the following assumptions:

- the annual salary will increase at the rate of inflation
- the safety net must be highly liquid in order to be a source of funds in the case of a financial emergency
- interest earned on the safety net will be enough to protect against loss of earning power due to inflation
- the safety net will be limited to three months salary
- a home equity line of credit will be established to provide funds should the safety net prove to be inadequate. Use of this line of credit should be considered as a last resort source of funds. It is not to be used as an ATM to fund one's basic lifestyle.
- all retirement contributions will be invested in an S&P 500 Index Mutual Fund or Exchange Traded Fund that will earn 12.0 percent, the average return from 1928–2005

- if actual rates of return from investments are lower than assumed in this strategy, the amount invested will be increased to compensate for the lower returns
- at retirement, 4 percent of the amount saved will be withdrawn annually. This means that at retirement twenty five times the annual salary at age 65 must have been accumulated in order to safely withdraw 4 percent annually to maintain the standard of living enjoyed before retirement and not outlive savings.

Phase I

Phase I of the Possible Retirement Strategy corresponds to the last two phases of the Young Adulthood Stage of Life's Progressions and covers ages thirty five to forty eight.

Phase I-A

Starting in Phase I-A, 10 percent of annual salary will be set aside to provide a safety net and save for retirement. Of the 10 percent annual savings, 25 percent will be placed in a liquid savings vehicle such as a passbook savings account or money market checking account. The remaining 75 percent that is allocated for retirement will be invested in an S&P 500 Index Exchange Traded Fund or Mutual Fund. It is critical for this strategy to succeed that a minimum of 10 percent of annual salary be set aside for saving at age thirty five or younger.

At the end of Phase I-A (age forty one), enough money would have been saved for the safety net to provide 2.1 months salary or 70 percent of the safety net goal of three months salary; 3.4 percent of the retirement goal of twenty five times annual salary.

PHASE I-A SAVINGS ACTIONS			
	• Establish a financial safety net of three months salary • Start saving for retirement fund of twenty five times annual income.	Percent of Goal	
Age		Safety Net	Retirement
Phase II of Young Adulthood Stage of Life's Progressions			
35	• Invest 2.5 percent of annual salary for safety net in a savings account or money market checking account each year. • Invest saving 7.5 percent of annual income for retirement in S&P 500 Index Fund or ETF.	10.0%	0.3%
36		20.0%	0.7%
37		30.0%	1.1%
38		40.0%	1.6%
39		50.0%	2.1%
40		60.0%	2.7%
41		70.0%	3.4%

It should be noted that saving more for retirement during Phase I of this strategy can produce dramatic results due to the effects of compounding.

Phase I-B

In Phase I-B, the safety net goal of three months annual salary is reached at age forty four. At age forty five, the 2.5 percent that was saved to provide a safety net is reallocated to saving for retirement. As a result, 10 percent of annual salary is saved for retirement.

At the end of Phase I-B, 11.4 percent of the retirement goal will have been saved. If one had not set aside more than 10 percent of his/her income for retirement or started saving before age thirty five, then his/her retirement fund would have longer for the impact of compound returns to have their effect. Conversely, starting later than thirty fiver or investing less for retirement will not allow one to be able to reach the retirement goal, of twenty five times annual earnings.

	PHASE I-B SAVINGS ACTIONS		
Age	• **Maintain safety net at three months salary** • **Continue saving for retirement fund of twenty five times annual income.**	**Percent of Goal**	
		Safety Net	**Retirement**
	Phase III of Young Adulthood Stage of Life's Progressions		
42	• Continue to invest 2.5 percent of annual salary for safety net in a savings account or money market checking account each year. • Continue saving 7.5 percent of annual income for retirement in S&P 500 Index Fund or ETF.	80.0%	4.1%
43		90.0%	5.0%
44		100.0%	5.9%
45	• Stop saving for safety net • Increase saving for retirement to 10.0 percent of annual salary. • Continue investing retirement funds in S&P 500	100.0%	7.1%
46		100.0%	8.3%
47		100.0%	9.8%
48		100.0%	11.4%

Phase II

Phase II covers the three phases of the Middle Age Stage of Life's Progression, ages forty nine to sixty five. Every year, 10 percent of annual salary is invested in the S&P 500. At age sixty five, the normal retirement age, one will have accumulated a retirement fund equal to twenty five times his/her annual salary. The critical factors in reaching this goal are to save at least 10 percent of annual salary each year and achieve a 12 percent rate of return from investing in the S&P 500 Index. It is strongly suggested that every effort be made to increase the saving rate whenever possible so as to provide a margin of safety for retirement.

PHASE II SAVINGS ACTIONS			
Age	• Maintain safety net at three months salary • Continue saving for retirement fund of twenty five times annual income.	**Percent of Goal**	
		Safety Net	Retirement
Phases I, II & III of Middle Age Stage of Life's Progressions			
49	• Continue saving 10.0 percent of annual income for retirement in S&P 500 Index Fund or ETF	100.0%	13.2%
50		100.0%	15.3%
51		100.0%	17.6%
52		100.0%	20.1%
53		100.0%	23.0%
54		100.0%	26.2%
55		100.0%	29.8%
56		100.0%	33.8%
57		100.0%	38.3%
58		100.0%	43.3%
9		100.0%	49.0%
60		100.0%	55.3%
61		100.0%	62.4%
62		100.0%	70.3%
63		100.0%	79.2%
64		100.0%	89.2%
65		100.0%	100.3%

Phase III

Unlike the Optimal Retirement Strategy, the Possible Retirement Strategy does not allow one to retire early or reach his/her retirement goal should returns on his/her investment be less than those assumed in this strategy.

As during the years of saving, the years of retirement require discipline. One should not splurge during the first years of retirement, but rather stick to the plan of withdrawing 4 percent of the retirement fund during the first year of retirement and adjusting the withdrawal rate by the rate of inflation every year thereafter.

The recommended approach for withdrawing funds for living expenses is analogous to the Optimal Retirement Strategy. It calls for having twelve months pre-retirement salary in a money market checking account, ten years in certificates of deposit and the balance in the S&P 500 Index.

- Upon retirement at age sixty five:
  - Transfer nine months salary from S&P 500 Index funds to a money market checking account. If the balance of the liquid asset portion of the safety net was placed in a savings account, then transfer that money into a money market checking account. This will provide twelve months of living expenses.
  - Transfer 120 months salary from the S&P 500 Index funds to certificates of deposit or Treasuries. The maturities should be laddered so that every month, one month's salary will mature and be ready for use if the money market checking account assets are not adequate to cover expenses. Together with the retirement funds that had been set aside for retirement previously this pool of money will represent ten years living expenses. As was the case with the Optimal Retirement Strategy, it is up to the individual investor to determine how much should be allocated to fixed income investments.
- Every year thereafter transfer twelve months salary adjusted for inflation from the S&P 500 Index funds to the money market checking account for living expenses.

Under this retirement strategy, one would not have to reduce his/her standard of living or outlive his/her money. In fact, the funds would continue to grow because the rate of return on these funds would exceed the rate of withdrawal from these funds. However, there would be less of a cushion than under the Optimal Retirement Strategy.

POSSIBLE RETIREMENT STRATEGY CASH FLOW

Age	Money Market Checking Account				Certificates of Deposit			S&P 500 Index Fund		
	Transfers	Withdrawals	Interest	Balance	Net Transfers	Interest	Balance	Transfers	Return	Balance
65				3.0			0.0			301.0
70	57	-60.0	NM	0.0	120.0	45.8	165.8	-177.0	114.8	238.8
75	60.0	-60.0	NM	0.0	0.0	63.3	229.1	-60.0	156.6	335.4
80	60.0	-60.0	NM	0.0	0.0	87.4	316.5	-60.0	230.3	505.7
85	60.0	-60.0	NM	0.0	0.0	120.8	437.4	-60.0	360.1	805.8
90	60.0	-60.0	NM	0.0	0.0	166.9	604.3	-60.0	588.8	1,334.6
95	60.0	-60.0	NM	0.0	0.0	230.7	835.0	-60.0	992.0	2,266.6
100	60.0	-60.0	NM	0.0	0.0	318.7	1153.7	-60.0	1,702.5	3,909.1

Under this scenario, one would have enough retirement funds to live until age ninety one in the unlikely case that during retirement one was not able to achieve a positive return on his/her retirement portfolio. Those who sacrificed to implement these guidelines and achieved the assumed rates of return on their investments would be able to reasonably expect to enjoy a retirement free from many financial worries.

Improbable Retirement Strategy

Phase I

The Improbable Retirement Strategy cannot achieve the retirement fund objective of twenty five times annual salary unless one is able to save 60 percent of his/her annual salary for retirement. Obviously, this is something that few among us would be able to do. Unlike the previous retirement strategies one only has ten years in which to save for retirement.

The Improbable Retirement Strategy is predicated on:
- one not being forced to retire prematurely
- annual increases in salary will be no less than the annual rate of inflation
- one invests 20 percent of his/her annual salary in the S&P 500 Index

- returns from the S&P 500 will average 12 percent per year, the average return from 1928 to 2005
- no safety net other than that which may have been saved prior to undertaking this retirement strategy. A home equity line of credit will be taken out to serve as a safety net
- there will not be an adequate retirement fund to allow for withdrawing 4 percent per year
- one compensates for insufficient retirement funds by working past age sixty five and/or reducing one's standard of living

By saving 20 percent of one's annual salary from ages fifty six to sixty five and investing that money in an S&P 500 Index Exchange Traded Fund or Mutual Fund, at age sixty five one would have accumulated a retirement fund equal to 47.1 months salary. It should be recognized by those who have undertaken this retirement strategy that they will have achieved a mere 15.7 percent of the amount needed to withdraw 4 percent of their retirement fund for the rest of their lives. This is certainly not a position one would knowingly want to be in.

PHASE I SAVINGS ACTIONS				
Age	• **Maintain no safety net** • **Start saving for retirement fund of twenty five times annual income.**		Percent of Goal	
			Safety Net	Retirement
Phase II & III of Middle Age Stage of Life's Progressions				
56	• Save 20.0 percent of annual income for retirement in S&P 500 Index Fund or ETF.		0.0%	0.9%
57			0.0%	1.9%
58			0.0%	3.0%
59			0.0%	4.3%
60			0.0%	5.7%
61			0.0%	7.3%
62			0.0%	9.0%
63			0.0%	11.0%
64			0.0%	13.2%
65			0.0%	15.7%

At the end of Phase I, one has reached the normal retirement age of sixty five.

Phase II

Unlike the previous two retirement strategies, the Improbable Retirement Strategy does not come close to be producing an adequate source of funds to maintain the standard of living enjoyed prior to retirement and not outlive the money saved. Basically those unfortunate to find themselves at age sixty five without having achieved their retirement savings goal would find themselves with two unpalatable options. These options are to:

- retire at age sixty five and reduce one's cost of living by 50 percent. This would mean that one would be able to withdraw only 2 percent of retirement funds each year rather than the 4 percent needed to preserve the standard of living enjoyed during the working years.

  This draconian action would require one to maintain one year's reduced expenditures in a Money Market Checking Account and the balance in an S&P 500 Index fund that would continue to earn 12 percent per year.

  Under this scenario one would have enough funds to live until age eighty one before running out of money.

- not retire at age sixty five and continue working until age seventy or seventy five and save 20 percent of annual salary for retirement. If one continued working until 70, he/she would have accumulated one hundred months salary; until seventy five, 194 months salary.

Returns on retirement assets would continue to earn the same rates of return in retirement as they did during working years. Upon retirement, one year's worth of the last year's annual salary would be maintained in a Money Market Checking account; one year worth in Certificates of Deposit; and any remaining funds would be invested in the S&P 500 Index. Each year, twelve months worth of salary would be transferred from the S&P 500 Index to the interest bearing checking account.

A person who worked until age seventy would be able to withdraw his/her inflation adjusted last annual salary from his/her retirement fund each year and exhaust his/her funds at age eighty. However working until age seventy five would allow that person to withdraw his/her inflation adjusted last annual salary from his/her retirement fund each year and not exhaust his/her funds until he/she was past one hundred.

This retirement strategy becomes even more untenable should one find themselves unable to work past age sixty five and unable to reduce his/her cost of living. The message here is to not under any circumstances allow oneself to be in this position. Don't expect some highly improbable, fortuitous event to provide for you in your retirement years. That rich relative you might have been depending on may decide to leave his/her estate to charity not to you.

Perhaps the Improbable Retirement Strategy should be referred to as the **PROBABLE RETIREMENT TRAGEDY**

INVESTING PRUDENTLY

For most people, investing in indexed funds is the optimal tradeoff between the potential rewards and risks of investing. The goal of most investors is to be able to sell at a price higher than their cost. Their goal should be to earn a rate of return that is not only greater than that offered by lower risk–lower reward investments but also compensates them for the level of risk associated with the investment. If one is not prepared to perform the necessary analyses to identify individual stocks to own, then that person would be best served by investing in funds indexed to the S&P 500 or other broad based indices.

There are four combinations of Risk-Reward combinations of possible investment opportunities that one might pursue.

1. **Low Risk-Low Reward**

   Low risk and low reward investments provide a relatively high degree of certainty that you will not lose your principal. However this, as with all things in life, comes at a price. These investments do not generally generate wealth. Rather they produce an income stream that hopefully will at least match the rate of inflation during the timeframe of the investment.

   Investments that fall in this Low Risk–Low Reward category include Treasury Bills, Certificates of Deposit, Treasury Notes, Treasury Bonds, Municipal Bonds and High Grade Corporate Bonds. When investing in such fixed income instruments, one should stagger or ladder the maturities to reduce undo exposure to dramatic changes in interest rates upon maturity.

2. **Low Risk–High Reward**

   Investing, as opposed to speculating, in equities has historically produced the best returns to investors over long periods of time. There is a wide range of equity related investments from which to choose. They range from broad based index funds to individual stocks.

   Unless one is willing to research thoroughly potential investments in individual stocks, the best way to invest in equities is through Mutual or Exchange Traded Funds that have lower fees. The more broadly diversified a fund is the lower the risk. Conversely, the more focused a fund the higher the potential rewards as wells as the risks. Broad based funds such as those indexed to the S&P 500 provide the safety of diversification coupled with annual returns that averaged 12.0 percent from 1928–2005. Investors wanting higher potential rewards must be cognizant of the fact that they would be undertaking commensurately higher risks.

3.   High Risk–High Reward

There are cases of investments that have both high risks and high rewards. An obvious example of one of these kinds of investments would be an individual who quits his job and places all his funds into a business he has founded in the hopes of developing a breakthrough technology that would revolutionize the world. While such an individual could potentially become another Bill Gates, the probability of such an achievement is miniscule. The probability of losing everything is almost 100 percent. Most of us, understanding the risks and rewards would not choose such an undertaking.

There are investments such as initial public offerings (IPOs), oil & gas partnerships, limited partnerships, venture capital funds, private equity funds, and hedge funds that provide individuals a vehicle to invest in High Risk–Reward opportunities. Those wishing to participate in such investments should do so with the expectation that they could sustain substantial losses. They should not invest in situations that are structured solely for the purpose of reducing taxes.

4.   High Risk–Low Reward

Investments with high risks and low rewards are not the kinds of investments that one would knowingly make. These so called "*opportunities of a lifetime*" usually guarantee you will lose a significant portion or the entire amount invested in such vehicles. An obvious example of this kind of an investment would be the Ponzi scheme. A less obvious example is that of trading in options, derivatives, or commodities. These vehicles allow knowledgeable traders to make huge sums of money. However, for the average investor the odds on making a profit are extremely low (Low Reward) and the odds of losing money are extremely high (High Risk).

**INVESTMENTS OFFERING RETURNS THAT ARE TOO
GOOD TO BE TRUE SHOULD ALWAYS BE AVOIDED. NEVER
EVEN CONSIDER HIGH RISK-LOW REWARD SITUATIONS.**

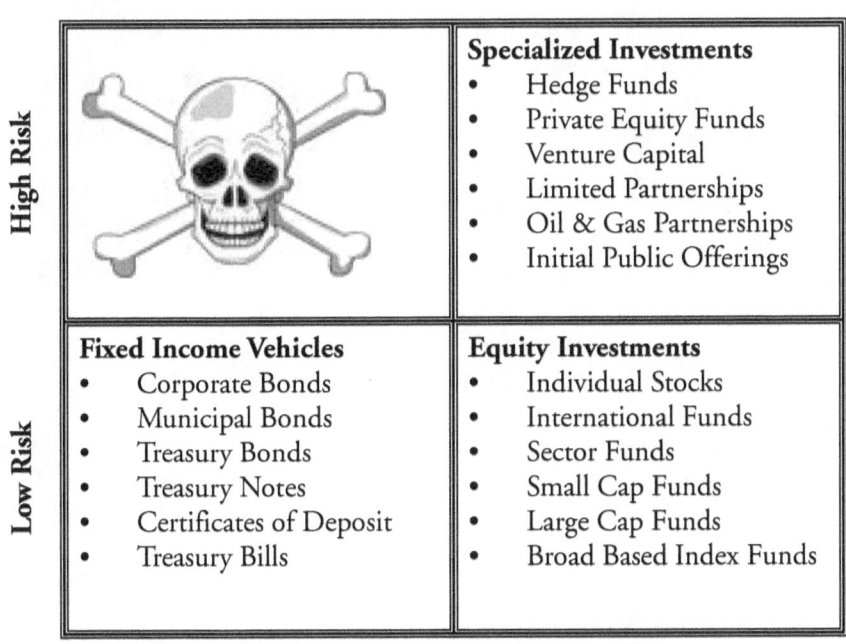

High Risk		**Specialized Investments** • Hedge Funds • Private Equity Funds • Venture Capital • Limited Partnerships • Oil & Gas Partnerships • Initial Public Offerings
Low Risk	**Fixed Income Vehicles** • Corporate Bonds • Municipal Bonds • Treasury Bonds • Treasury Notes • Certificates of Deposit • Treasury Bills	**Equity Investments** • Individual Stocks • International Funds • Sector Funds • Small Cap Funds • Large Cap Funds • Broad Based Index Funds
	Low Reward	**High Reward**

Concepts to Consider

Asset Allocation

The purpose of allocating a predetermined proportion of assets among various types of investments is to minimize risk. It is based on the concept that at over any given period of time certain assets classes will outperform others. A proper asset allocation can increase the likelihood of achieving an investor's goals despite the underperformance of a portion of his/her assets. In order to be effective, the returns from the different asset classes should not be dependent on similar factors. An asset allocation of 50 percent in oil stocks and 50 percent in oil itself would not provide protection against a drop in oil prices.

The more common forms of asset classes are:

- Cash
  - ○ Money Market Funds
  - ○ Savings Accounts
- Bonds
  - ○ Government vs. Corporate
  - ○ Investment Grade vs. Junk
  - ○ Short-term vs. Medium-term vs. Long-term
  - ○ Domestic vs. Foreign
- Stocks
  - ○ Large-Cap vs. Mid-Cap vs. Small-Cap
  - ○ Growth vs. Value
  - ○ Domestic vs. Foreign
- Real Estate
  - ○ Residential vs. Commercial
  - ○ Real Estate Investment Trusts (REIT) vs. direct ownership
- Other
  - ○ Foreign Currency
  - ○ Natural Resources
  - ○ Precious Metals
  - ○ Collectibles
  - ○ Etc.

Diversification

Diversification, like Asset Allocation, is based on the concept that a group of different investments will, on average, produce higher returns and lower the risk than any individual investment within the portfolio. The performance of the winners will more than compensate for the losers.

Diversification often is used to refer to the degree of concentration within a particular class of assets. For example, within the portion of a portfolio allocated to stocks, it refers to the impact a particular stock or group of stocks will have on the performance of the stock portion of the portfolio. In order to have a diversified portfolio of an asset class such as stocks, one would ideally need twenty five to thirty stocks. For most investors, their limited funds preclude them from achieving this level of diversification when investing in individual stocks. These individuals would be best served by investing the equity portion of their portfolios in a low cost, tax efficient index fund.

While diversification limits the downside risk, it also limits the upside potential. With a portfolio of twenty five stocks, each stock would represent 4 percent of the portfolio's value. In order to maximize the returns of the portfolio, one would want to own a higher percentage of the best performing stocks and a lower percentage of the worst ones. Successful investors accomplish this by not mechanically adhering to a diversification model that requires each stock to represent a fixed percentage of the portfolio. Rather they allow the best performers to dominate their portfolios without losing the benefits of diversification. As a general rule of thumb one should not allow a single stock or group of stocks in the same industry to account for more than 10 to 15 percent of the value of the equity portion of their portfolio. Having twenty five semiconductor stocks in the equity portion of a portfolio provides minimal if any diversification as they will all tend to do well and poorly more due to industry trends rather than company specific events.

Internal Rate of Return

In order to be successful as an investor, one must know how to measure the profitability of an investment. An investor who purchased 100 shares of the Alpha Company for $10.00 per share and sold all one hundred shares for $12.00 per share might consider the $2.00 per share profit to be a return of 20.0 percent. The validity of that assumption is based on the length of time the investor held those 100 shares. If the shares were held for twelve months, then indeed that would represent a return of 20.0 percent on the original investment (ROI). Were those same shares held for ten years, the ROI would still be 20 percent but the investment would have been less profitable since it earned an average of 2.0 percent per year.

Many stock investments are held for the long term and pay dividends to the investor. The amount of the annual dividend can vary over time. Over time additional shares may be acquired at different costs. The calculation of Return on Investment partially addresses these cases. However, as should be apparent to the reader of this book, it is important to factor in the time horizon of an investment in determining its profitability. Whether one earns 20 percent over one year or 10 years is critical in creating wealth for oneself. If the returns were achieved in the first year of a multi year investment or the last year is critical.

A method that can be used to account for the timing of the costs and returns from an investment is called the Internal Rate of Return, a technique that has been typically used to evaluate capital budgeting decisions by corporations but can also be used to measure the profitability of an investment. The following example illustrates the differences between Return on Investment (ROI) and Internal Rate of Return (IRR).

Let us assume that one hundred shares of the Alpha Company's stock are purchased for $10.00 per share. At the end of ten years, the shares are sold for $15.00

per share. Under this scenario the ROI is 50 percent while the IRR is 4.1 percent. The profitability of the investment varies widely depending on the yardstick used for measurement.

Dividend Reinvestment

Dividend Reinvestment is when the dividends received from a stock are used to purchase additional shares in the stock of that company. The ability of these dividends to generate additional earnings from additional dividend payments and appreciation in the price of the stock is a phenomenon referred to as compound returns. Investors who do not reinvest their dividends are missing out on an opportunity to increase the returns from their investments.

Dollar Cost Averaging

Despite our best efforts, we cannot always buy stocks at the lowest price. By investing a fixed amount of money on a regular basis, it is possible to reduce the risk of buying a large amount of stock at the wrong price. When the price of the stock is high less shares will be bought than when the price per share is low. By dollar cost averaging one can reduce the cost basis of a stock position.

Dividend Reinvestment is a form of Dollar Cost Averaging. The dividends are paid at fixed intervals and are a relatively fixed amount of money subject to dividend rate increases of decreases.

Let us examine two options for purchasing shares of stock. Under Option A, one hundred shares of stock are bought at one time for $10.00 per share and sold later for $9.00 per share. Option A would have produced a loss of $1.00 per share.

OPTION A			
Action	Shares	Cost/ Share	Ave Cost
Buy 100 shares @ 10.00 for a total cost of $1,000	100.00	10.00	10.00
Sell 100 shares @ 9.00			
LOSS		100.00	

Under Option B, equal purchases of $200 are spread over five time periods. Under this approach, 115.75 shares would have been bought with an average cost per share of $8.64. Liquidating the position at $9.00 per share would produce a profit of $81.67 as compared to a loss of $100.00 under Option A.

OPTION B			
Action	Shares	Cost/ Share	Ave Cost
Buy $200 worth of stock @ 10.00	20.00	10.00	10.00
Buy $200 worth of stock @ 9.00	22.22	9.00	9.47
Buy $200 worth of stock @ 8.00	25.00	8.00	8.93
Buy $200 worth of stock @ 8.50	23.53	8.50	8.82
Buy $200 worth of stock @ 8.00	25.00	8.00	8.64
TOTAL	115.75		
Sell 115.75 shares @ 9.00			
PROFIT		**81.67**	

Dollar Cost Averaging would not have been a good idea if the price of the stock had increased rather than decreased.

While frequently used as a tool for reducing the risk of buying at too high a price, Dollar Cost Averaging can also be used to reduce the risk of having sold at too low a price. Under this scheme, an investor would sell a fixed dollar amount of stock at predetermined intervals. When the price per share was high less shares would be sold than when the price was low.

While Dollar Cost Averaging has been discussed in terms of stocks, it can and should be used when buying stock funds.

Reversion to the Mean

Reversion to the Mean, as used in statistics, states that "*the greater the deviation of a random variate from its mean the greater the probability that the next measured variate will deviate less far.*" As applied to equity markets, it states that the equities market will return to its average valuation level. Markets that overvalue equities as well as those that undervalue equities will revert to their average valuation.

Unlike the statistical assumption upon which the concept of Reversion to the Mean is based, changes in stock valuations are not a result of random factors. Rather they are based on investor perceptions of variables such as the direction of the economy, interest rates, inflation, company earnings, the impact of innovation, changes in competitiveness, etc. and their impact on the value investors will assign to a stock. The challenge for the investor is to determine the appropriate measure(s) of value and the average valuation measure(s) against which to compare.

Identifying Stocks to Buy

Before there can be a discussion on identifying stocks to buy, there must be a clear understanding of the rationale for investing in individual stocks. Inherent in the decision to invest in individual stocks is the belief that over the long term it is possible to achieve a higher rate of return than can be achieved from alternative investment opportunities. Implicit in the decision to invest in individual stocks is the commitment to thoroughly analyze potential investments and to continually monitor the progress of the stock, its company, its industry as well as economic and geopolitical events that could have a favorable or unfavorable impact on them.

There are several sources of information that can be used to identify potential stock investments. They include television pundits, newspaper and magazine articles, conversations with acquaintances, recommendation of financial advisors, stock screeners, etc. However, despite the source of a potential investment, it is critical that the disciplined investor perform his/her own due diligence.

A stock that should be considered as a potential investment has certain characteristics that make it attractive. It should have:

- **Strong Competitive Advantages**

    Competitive advantage can take many forms. It may manifest itself as high barriers to entry for new competitors, strong brand recognition by consumers, highly efficient supply chain management, strong patent protection, reputation for innovation, high quality products, high customer dependency, de facto industry standard, financial assets, management strength, technological leadership, operational execution, unique products and/or services, reputation for excellence, etc. It allows a company to outperform its peers and prohibit new entrants into its markets from succeeding. These companies are not complacent with their performance and can be almost paranoid in their endeavors to continue to excel. They do not view innovation as a threat but rather as an opportunity. They strike a balance between short term and longer term objectives.

- o **3M Company** recognized for its innovation and manufacturing excellence
- o **Adobe Systems** its Portable Document Format (PDF) software is a de facto industry standard with high costs for user to switch from.
- o **Amazon.com** dominates the online retail space.
- o **Amgen** biotech industry leader with several blockbuster drugs and a deep pipeline of new drugs under development
- o **Applied Materials** is the industry leader with a broad product line and technological leadership.
- o **Boeing Co** competes in an oligopoly with Airbus who faces operational and product development issues.
- o **Coca Cola** benefits from having one of the world's most recognized brands and a global distribution network.
- o **eBay** created and dominates the online auction market.
- o **Equifax** operates in an oligopoly market that has high barriers to entry
- o **Exxon-Mobil** world's largest and most efficient oil producer.
- o **General Electric** dominates many of its markets and is known for the strength of its management.
- o **Google** synonymous with Internet search and is often used as a verb.
- o **Harley-Davidson** internationally recognized brand
- o **Medtronic** dominates the medical equipment market with its broad array of products and technological leadership position.
- o **Microsoft** dominates the PC software market with products that have high costs for customers to switch from.
- o **PepsiCo** dominates the salty snack business and has the number position two in the beverages sector. Has a highly effective distribution model.
- o **Pitney Bowes** dominates the worldwide market for postage meters.
- o **Proctor & Gamble** owns some of the world's most recognized consumer products many of which have annual sales in excess of $1 billion.
- o **Qualcomm** owner of significant intellectual property for wireless communications industry

- **Teva Pharmaceutical** world's largest generic drug manufacturer
- **Toyota Motors** recognized for the quality of its cars and efficiency of its operations.
- **Wal-Mart** has one of the world's most efficient supply chain management systems. Reputation for providing low cost products to the consumer
- **Western Union** dominates the money market transfer business. Its brand is recognized and trusted worldwide.

As the above listed of companies illustrates, competitive advantages can take different forms. The disciplined investor must develop an understanding of a company's competitive advantages and disadvantages before purchasing its stock. The information needed to develop the competitive position of a company can be obtained from:

- The company's annual reports
- SEC filings
- Newspapers such as the Wall Street Journal, Investors Business Daily and Barron's
- Magazines such Business Week, Forbes, and Fortune
- Industry publications
- Research reports such as those prepared by Morningstar, Standard & Poor's, Argus Research, Reuters Research, Goldman Sachs, Charles Schwab, Fidelity Investments, Lehman Bros., Merrill Lynch, etc.
- Internet sites such as Yahoo Finance, CNN Money, and CNBC

As one can see there are numerous sources of information regarding a potential investment in a company. With easy access to this information, it is totally inexcusable for anyone to take a position in a company without doing his/her homework.

Those who skimp on the research are not disciplined investors. They are not even speculators. They are gamblers who don't even understand the odds of succeeding. They merely place their bets and wait for the roulette wheel to stop.

An understanding of the competitive position of a company in of itself is insufficient information upon which to make a well thought-out investment. One must also understand the company's financial position.

- **Sound Financial Position**

    The financial position of a company for the purposes of this book is its profitability, the financial resources at its disposal, and the effectiveness in which it manages its assets. Fortunately for the disciplined investor there are many well accepted measures that have been developed in the field of Finance. These measures include:

o **Investment Return**
  - **Return on Equity (ROE)** *(ratio of Net Profits to Equity)*. This percentage represents the returns to investors.
  - **Return on Invested Capital (ROI)** *(ratio of Net Income less Dividends to Total Capital)*. It is a measure of how efficiently a company is able to utilize its capital structure. Unless ROI exceeds a company's cost of capital, it is not effectively running its operations.
  - **Return on Assets (ROA)** *(ratio of Net Income to Total Assets)*. It is a measure of how profitably a company utilizes its assets.
o **Price Ratios**
  - **Revenue per Share** *(ratio of Annual Revenues to weighted Average Number of Shares Outstanding)*. The higher the ratio the better. It is sometimes used to value companies that are not operating at a profit.
  - **Book Value per Share** *(Total Shareholder Equity less Preferred Equity divided by Total Shares Outstanding)*. It represents the liquidation value of each share of common stock.
  - **Price/Earnings Ratio** *(Price per Share divided by the 12 month Earnings per Share)*. It represents how much investors are willing to pay for each dollar of earnings.
  - **Price to Book Value** *(ratio of Stock Price to Total Assets (net of Intangible Assets and Liabilities))*. It indicates the value of a company to an investor in a company with meager growth prospects.
  - **Price/Sales Ratio** *(Price per Share divided by the 12 month Sales per Share)*. It represents how much investors are willing to pay for each dollar of revenues.
  - **Price/Cash Flow Ratio** *(Share Price divided by Cash Flow per Share)*. Cash flow removes depreciation and other non cash charges from net earnings. The Price/Cash Flow Ratio is another metric for valuing a share of common stock.
o **Management Efficiency**
  - **Revenue per Employee** *(12 month Revenues divided by weighted average Number of Employees)*. It is a measure of how productively a company utilizes its workforce to generate revenues.

- **Income per Employee** *(ratio of 12 month Income to the weighted number of Employees)*. It is a measure of how productive a company is in utilizing its workforce to generate income.
- **Receivables Turnover** *(ratio of Net Credit Sales to Average Accounts Receivable)*. A measure of a company's effectiveness in collecting on its credit sales. The higher the number the better.
- **Inventory Turnover** *(ratio of Cost of Goods Sold to Average Inventory)*. It is a measure of how effectively a company manages its inventory levels in relation to its sales levels.
- **Asset Turnover** *(ratio of Revenues to Total Assets)*. The higher the ratio, the more effectively a company uses its assets in supporting its sales levels.

o **Financial Condition**
- **Current Ratio** *(ratio of Current Assets to Current Liabilities)*. It is a measure of a company ability to meet its current obligations. A high ratio can indicate that the company has more than enough assets that can be liquidated, if needed, to safely meet its short obligations. On the other hand, an excessively high current ratio can also be interpreted as an inefficient use of resources on the part of management.
- **Quick Ratio** *(ratio of Current Assets minus Inventory to Current Liabilities)*. The Quick Ratio is also referred to as the Liquidity Ratio or . It is a more stringent test of a company's ability to meets its current liabilities. The reason for excluding inventory is that often the book value of inventory may not be readily realized in the event of a forced liquidation. As a general rule the Quick Ratio is expected to be 1:1. A value much less than one can be a red flag.
- **Debt to Equity Ratio or Leverage** *(ratio of Total Debt to Total Equity)*. It assesses the relative portion of debt to the capital structure of a company. A high ratio indicates the use of a preponderance of debt in financing the company and the risk of the company not being able to cover its debt obligations. A high ratio will produce a more significant percentage increase or decrease in earnings per share than a low ratio.

- ♦ **Interest Coverage** *(ratio of Earnings Before Interest and Taxes (EBIT) to the Annual Interest Expense on a company's outstanding debt)*. It is a measure of the degree of safety there is for a company to cover its interest expense. A ratio of less than 1.5:1 might call into question a company's ability to pay its interest expense.
- o **Growth Rates** Positive rates of growth in both earnings per shares and revenue are indicative of a company that is continuing to grow profitably over various time frames. The growth in earnings should be at least that of the rate of growth in revenues.
- o **Profits Margins**
  - ♦ **Gross Margin** *(Gross Revenues minus Cost of Goods Sold)*. It is often expressed as a percentage of sales. Gross Margin indicates the amount of money available to cover fixed costs and contribute to profits.
  - ♦ **Pre-Tax Margin** *(profits after deducting fixed costs and before deducting taxes expressed as a percent of sales)*. Due to the potential volatility of tax rates from year to year this gives a clearer picture of the items that are within the control of the company's management.
  - ♦ **Net Profit Margin** *(profits after deducting taxes and all other charges expressed as a percent of sales)*. This is a measure of the effectiveness of management in running all aspects of the business.
- o **Current Financials**
  - ♦ **Revenues** from continuing operations and discontinued operations must be differentiated in order to evaluate a company's ability to grow its business.
  - ♦ **Earnings per Share** from continuing operations and discontinued operations must be differentiated in order to evaluate a company's ability to profitably grow its business.

- **Payouts to Investors** come in two forms, dividends and stock repurchases. Companies with a history of increasing their dividends and share repurchases can be attractive to the long term investor.
- **Analyst Projections** are an important factor in determining the advisability of investing in the stock of a company. Since the average investor does not have the ability to independently obtain the information necessary to project

the prospects of a company, he/she has no choice but to rely on the projections of the analysts who follow a stock

The issue for the disciplined investor is not a dearth of financial data to use in formulating a decision to invest in the stock of a company but rather a plethora of information. One of the best ways for sorting through the quantitative data on a company's current and projected performance is through the use of a stock screener.

It cannot be emphasized enough that stock screeners are a tool to be used in deciding whether or not to invest in a particular stock. The stock may be a good one to own but its current price may fully reflect its anticipated performance and thus may not be a suitable candidate for the disciplined investor's portfolio. Discipline requires that stocks are not purchased unless their current price discounts their future prospects of the company. There are 2 fundamental questions that investors should ask when evaluating potential stock investments.

1.   Does the company meet my evaluation criteria?
2.   What is a reasonable price to pay for it?

Before one can use a stock screener, one must identify what is the yardstick against which stocks should be evaluated. Some choose the S&P 500 Index as that yardstick, others the Russell 2000, Dow Jones Industrial Average, etc. Since there is a large disparity between companies that comprise these and other benchmarks due to the idiosyncrasies of their industries, using the company's industry as the benchmark may make more sense. Since some industries have different characteristics such as high capital costs (utilities), low margins (food retailers), high sensitivity to fuel costs (airlines), rapid technological innovation (semiconductors), etc., it is more reasonable to compare apples to apples, companies within a specific industry to each other.

The S&P 500 Index is comprised of ten sectors, each of which is divided into industry groups which in turn are divided into industries. An examination of the S&P 500 at the end of the first quarter of 2005 would reveal that that the index had a Price to Earnings ratio (P/E) of 20, 7.3 percent Return on Invested Capital (ROI), 14.0 percent Return on Equity (ROE), and a five year growth rate in equity of 11 percent and Earnings per Share (EPS) of 7 percent. However, there were wide variations in these numbers within the ten sectors comprising the S&P 500 Index.

A comparison of the Energy Sector to the S&P 500 Composite reveals that based on Return on Invested Capital and Equity as well as five year growth in Equity and Earnings per Share, the Energy Sector traded at a significantly lower Price-to-Earnings Ratio. Going one step further, the Oil, Gas & Consumables industry had higher returns and growth than the Energy Sector yet had a lower P/E Ratio.

1st Quarter 2005 S&P Selected Measures				5 Yr Growth	
	ROI	ROE	P/E	Equity	EPS
ALL-INDUSTRY COMPOSITE	7.3	14.0	20	11	7
Consumer Discretionary	3.7	8.0	32	13	7
Consumer Staples	13.5	22.3	20	11	10
Energy	16.6	22.2	13	18	19
Financials	5.7	13.6	14	15	8
Health Care	12.2	15.7	27	20	11
Industrials	6.3	12.8	23	10	6
Information Technology	13.3	15.9	25	8	1
Materials	7.3	14.4	18	5	4
Telecommunication Services	2.2	4.6	53	-8	-5
Utilities	4.4	10.8	19	7	1

Data: *Business Week*

Since the returns and growth rates of Murphy Oil are higher than the S&P 500 Composite yet have a lower P/E Ratio, sixteen versus twenty, one might conclude that it is undervalued. However, if it is compared against its peers in the Oil & Gas Consumable Fuels Industry, it is an underperformer with a P/E Ratio significantly higher than its industry peers.

1st Quarter 2005 S&P Selected Measures				5 Yr Growth	
	ROI	ROE	P/E	Equity	EPS
ALL-INDUSTRY COMPOSITE	7.3	14.0	20	11	7
Energy	16.6	22.2	13	18	19
Oil, Gas & Consumable Fuels	17.8	23.6	11	20	21
Murphy Oil	16.2	20.0	16	19	18

Data: *Business Week*

In order to use a stock screener, the selection criteria must be carefully determined. Investors must choose the criteria that are important to them. Most investors want some combination of:

- **Investment Return** as measured by Returns on Equity, Assets and Invested Capital
- **Price Ratios** such as Price-to-Book Value, Price-to-Earnings Ratio, Price-to-Sales Ratio, Price-to-Cash Flow Ratio, Book Value per Share, and Price-to-Earnings Growth
- **Management Efficiency** as measured by Revenue and Income per Employee, as well as Receivables, Inventory and Asset Turnover
- **Financial Position** as measured by Debt/Equity Ratio, Current Ratio, Quick Ratio, Interest Coverage, Leverage Ratio, etc.
- **Profit Margins** such as Gross, Pre-Tax and Net Profit
- **Returns to Investors** in the form of Dividends and Stock Repurchase Programs
- **Growth Rates** of Dividends, Earnings per Share, and Revenue
- **Analysts Projections and Ratings**

Investors use these factors to determine the relationship between them and the stocks current and historical pricing. In order to perform this, one would have to transfer the results from the stock screener into a spreadsheet in which the detailed analysis could be performed. A methodology for doing this is to rate a company's performance against each criterion on a one to ten scale. Then assign each of the criteria a weighting factor according to the relative importance of each parameter in the decision process. A reasonable way to assign weights is as follows:

0.   No Importance Whatsoever
1.   Minor Importance
2.   Minor–Moderate Importance

3. Moderate Importance
4. Moderate–Major Importance
5. Major Importance

For each criterion, multiply the score times the associated weighting factor and then add the score-weighting factor of each criterion to get a total weighted score. The final step of this analysis is to force rank each stock's total weighted score in descending order. This will put the stock with the highest ranking, the one that best satisfies your set of criteria, at the top of the list. This completes the quantitative portion of the analysis.

Interpreting the validity of the quantitative analyses for selecting potential stock investments is difficult unless there is a clear understanding of a company's strategic position in the markets in which it competes. One must understand each company's strengths and weaknesses and the unique challenges it faces. In addition, one should understand the barriers to entry that potential competitors must surmount. This can best be done by studying a company's annual report, SEC filings, and articles written about it. After completing this analysis, one should compare the results against the quantitative analyses of each company and determines whether or not to invest in the company.

Investors need to remember that stock analysts and many other sources of stock recommendations are focused on near term results. As a disciplined investor, one must remember that your goals are longer term. Blindly following the market pundits, you will most likely be buying high in the hopes of selling higher. At some point in the cycle of escalating stock prices the music stops and the stock's price will drop. Unfortunately, nobody can tell when that will happen with any degree of certainty. To illustrate this point, let us examine the price history of Sirius Satellite Radio. Those who were fortunate enough to have bought in Dec 1996 when the stock sold at $4.13 per share and sold in Oct 2000 when the stock sold at $52.88 would have profited handsomely while the company's fundamentals subsequently deteriorated. From 1996 to 2000, Cash Flow went from (0.27) per share to (4.66) per share and losses from 0.27 per share to 4.72 per share. However, those who did not sell the stock saw its price deteriorate to 0.64 in Dec 2002. By Nov 2005, the stock had seen its price appreciate to $7.15 per share. This was small consolation to investors who had purchased and held the stock from 1997 to 2001 when the stock traded for over $10.00 per share.

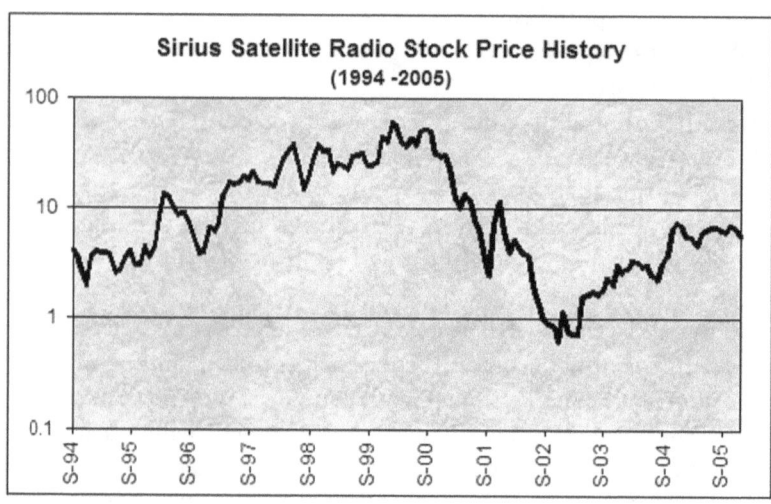

Fig. 6-1 Stock price history of Sirius Satellite Radio from 1994–2005
Data *Yahoo Finance*

Assuming that the quantitative and qualitative analyses indicate that a stock satisfies your purchase criteria, then you must determine whether the stock is undervalued. This is done by comparing the company's price to its historical relationship to the price ratios and other parameters used in identifying the stock for potential purchase. If the relationship between the stock's price and these measures is less than its historical mean and its fundamentals are positive, then consider a purchase. Just because a stock is cheap does not mean that it cannot become cheaper. Often when buying a stock that it is undervalued, one should not be surprised to see its price fall. Therefore, when buying such a stock, one should determine the amount of money to invest and then divide that amount into three or four purchases spread out over a couple of months. Before each investment reconfirm the advisability of purchasing the stock. By dividing the purchases into fixed dollar amounts, one can take advantage of dollar cost averaging. If the company's prospects have deteriorated, one should consider not purchasing or delaying the purchase of additional shares. If the deterioration is significant, a sale of the stock should be considered.

Remember that when buying undervalued stocks, you are making a long term investment and that short term price declines, while potentially painful, in of themselves are not a reason to panic. If the company's strategic competitive position remains strong, one should view price declines as opportunities to purchase additional shares and to lower the average costs of his/her investment in that stock. Many industries are cyclical and investing in them when they are out of favor can be an excellent way of achieving meaningful returns. The issue with out of favor or undervalued stocks is to determine whether the condition is temporary or a seismic shift in the stock's prospects.

In 1998, the price per barrel of oil had fallen to $11.91, the lowest price in twenty years. Those industries such as transportation, utilities, and chemicals certainly benefited from the lower price of one of their significant cost components. However, as with most things, there were other industries, most notably those involved in the exploration for oil, which suffered from the low price of oil. Given the lack of financial incentives, certain oil prospects became uneconomical to pursue.

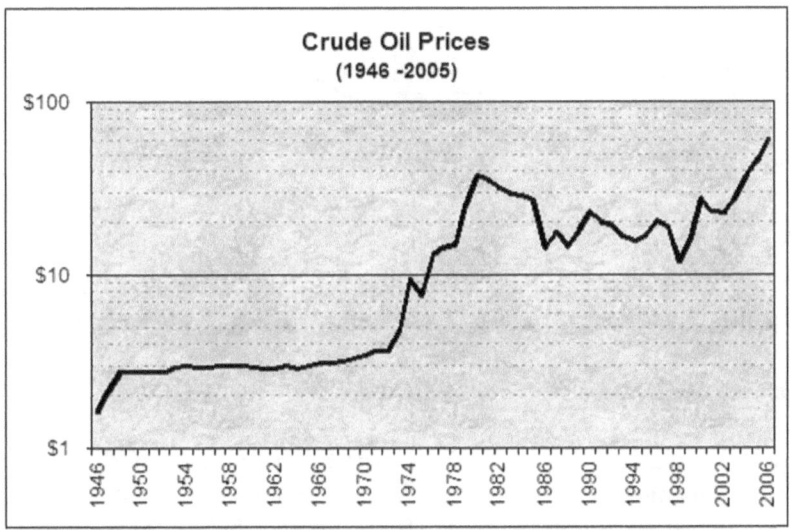

Fig. 6-2 Crude Oil Prices per Barrel from 1946—2005
Data: *United States Department of Energy*

Those who understood that these low oil prices were an aberration invested in companies that would benefit from a firmer pricing environment. One such company was Apache Corporation, an oil & gas exploration, development, and production company operating primarily in the United States. From 1998 to 2005, its revenues increased from $876 million to $7,548 million, its net income from a loss of $129 million to a profit of $2,624 million. Its returns on assets and equity increased to 15.1 percent and 28.2 percent respectively. As a result, Apache's stock price increased from $7.92 in 1998 to $75.13 in 2005. As the following chart demonstrates there is a direct correlation between the price of crude oil and the stock performance of oil & gas companies such as Apache. Few were raising the buy signs for oil & gas companies in 1998. But disciplined value investors recognized that the stock market was having a sale on companies in that industry.

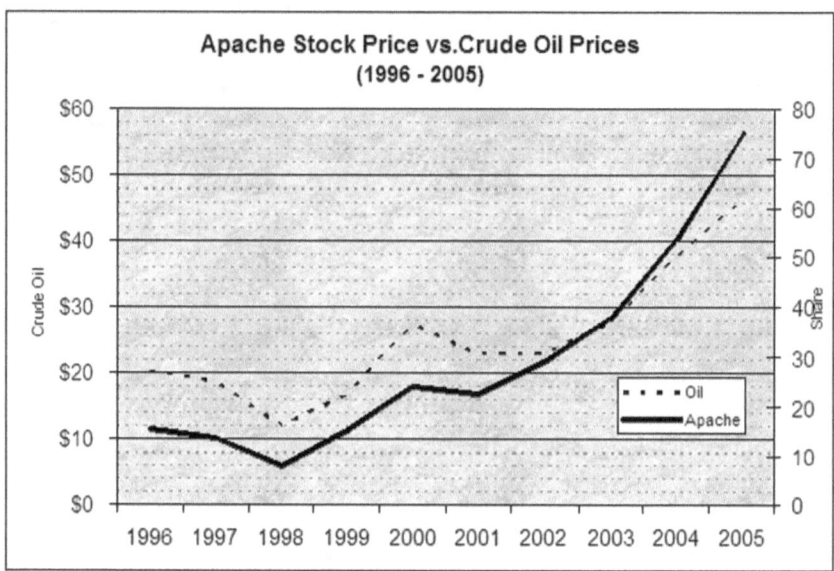

Fig. 6-3 Relationship of crude oil prices per barrel to the price per share of Apache Corp common stock from 1996—2005
Data: *United States Department of Energy Yahoo Finance*

From 1998 to 2005, Exxon Mobil Corporation, the behemoth of the integrated oil companies, saw its revenues increase from $117.8 billion to $370.7 billion and its net income from $6.4 billion to $36.1 billion. During that same time period its Return on Assets went from 6.8 percent to 17.9 percent and its Return on Equity from 14.8 percent to 33.9 percent. Exxon Mobil's share price went from $24.17 to $57.17. Shareholders over that same time period would have received cumulative dividends of $6.73 per share. It is interesting to note that this company has a history of increasing its annual dividends even during times of challenging industry conditions. Despite the decline in oil prices, this company increased dividends from $0.78 per share in 1996 to $1.14 in 2005.

Disciplined investors must determine for themselves whether or not to adopt the contrarian strategy of investing in out of favor value stocks. Remember, unlike a track meet, there is no starter's gun that signals investors to buy and there is also no finish line that says sell.

Once the decision has been made to purchase a stock, the best way to execute the transaction is through the on-line systems of discount brokers such as Charles

Schwab and Fidelity Investment. These companies offer a wide range of research tools and low costs of doing business for investors. When executing a buy order, do not place a Market Order but instead a Limit Order in which you specify the maximum price you are willing to pay for the number of shares that you want. Limit Orders protect the investor from paying more than his/her target price. If the stock remains above your Limit Order price, revaluate your limit price and either adjust the price upward you are willing to pay or move on to the next investment opportunity. If the stock pays a dividend, then enroll it in the broker's dividend reinvestment program to take advantage of potential compound returns.

The disciplined investor should not lose sight of his/her goal which is to buy a stock at a price that produces a return greater that that which could have been achieved from an index such as the S&P 500.

Identifying Stocks to Sell

Before one can identify stocks that should be sold, one must understand the rationale for such a transaction. Most reasons for selling a stock can be divided into three categories:

1. Company's prospects have deteriorated

The company has failed to meet earnings expectations, its principal competitor has gained market share at its expense, customers are cutting back on their orders, there are unexpected senior management departures, its products are suspected of having a deleterious effect on customers, etc. Any one of these may cause a company's prospects to deteriorate. Constantly keeping abreast of company and industry events as they unfold can help determine whether the problems are temporary or indicate a long term impediment to the company's long term success.

There are certain situations such as accounting irregularities, a pattern of supposed one time restructuring charges, governmental investigations, elimination of dividends, significant management turnover, etc. that often indicate that the company's long term outlook may be in question. In such a situation, determine the lowest price that you would sell the stock for and place a Stop Loss Order at that price. Such an action can allow you to achieve a modicum of downside protection. If the stock climbs in price, increase the Stop Loss Price to increase returns from the investment.

2. More attractive investment opportunities are identified.

Most investors have limited funds with which to invest. In order to make an investment, they sometimes have to liquidate one or more other investments. Compare the potential investment with existing equity investments to determine where it stands in comparison with the existing ones. Those stocks that have less promising prospects are candidates for sale.

All things being equal, non dividend paying stocks should be sold before dividend payers. Rather than eliminating an entire stock position in a company, it may be better to sell partial positions in the stock of more than one company. Be sure that the changes in your portfolio that result from swapping stocks in one or more companies in your portfolio for new positions does not appreciably alter the planned sector allocations of your equity positions.

3. Funds are needed for non investment purposes.

In the case where funds are needed for something other than to make an investment, one must distinguish between a one time and a reoccurring need.

If the need is reoccurring, suspend dividend reinvestments in stocks held in taxable accounts and use those payments to cover your needs. If that action is insufficient or the need is a one time occurrence, then consider liquidating the stocks that have the least promising prospects.

Just because a stock has performed well in the past, does not mean that it should not be subject to the same rigorous analysis that was used in deciding to take a position in that stock. Stocks are inanimate objects and keeping stocks with poor prospects for sentimental reasons is not something that the disciplined investor would do. Remember that a stock's price is based on the expectations of its performance in the future not the past.

While taxes and dividends should not be a consideration in liquidating an equity position, the timing of the transaction can be important if:

- Delaying the sale transforms a short term capital gain into a long term one with a lower capital gains tax rate
- Accelerating the sale preserves a short term capital loss that can be used as an offset against income.
- Timing the transaction to capitalize on the Ex-Dividend Date so as to receive a dividend payment that might not otherwise be received based on the date of the stock transaction.

While dollar cost averaging is usually thought of as a tool to be utilized when buying a stock, it can also be used when selling one. Instead of selling the entire position in a stock at once, sell equal dollar amounts at fixed intervals of time. Obviously, when there is a need for the entire amount at one time this technique is of limited value.

In summary, the time to sell a stock is when the risks of keeping it outweigh the rewards of keeping it or there are other investment opportunities that have a better risk/reward profile.

Managing an Investment Portfolio

An integral part of managing an investment portfolio is to have the materials necessary to track its performance and identify opportunities for improvement. Disciplined investors not only analyze potential additions to their portfolio but also apply a similar rigor in the analysis of their holdings. They rely on:

- **Comprehensive Inventory of Assets**

    Investors need to understand all the assets in their investment portfolio. The inventory's purpose is to consolidate in one place a complete listing of the assets comprising the investment portfolio. Whether this inventory is in a ledger sheet, spreadsheet, or accounting system is irrelevant. The minimal information in an inventory of holdings is the same.

    For fixed income assets, the information should include type of instrument (CD, T-Bill, T-Note, T-Bill, Corporate Bond, etc.), issuer (Bank, US Treasury, Company, etc.), maturity date, account or other identification number and face value. In the case of equities, the information should include type of equity (ETF, Mutual Fund, Common Stock, etc.), company name, and number of shares.

    It should be noted that the use of personal computer based software can eliminate duplicate data entry and reconciliation problems inherent in manual paper based systems.

- **Accurate Accounting of Costs and Returns of each Asset**

    It is important to keep track of the income generated from investments and the associated costs for income tax purposes and just as importantly to provide the data needed to assess the performance of an investment portfolio. For each asset, a description of the asset, the quantities bought and sold, cost basis and sale price, dividend and interest payments, dividend reinvestments, maturity dates, and the dates of each transaction should be recorded ideally using personal computer software. This information will be essential in preparing tax returns and measuring the performance of the investment portfolio.

- **Monitoring Returns from each Holding**

     It is essential for disciplined investors to know the returns each of their investments produce based on their actual costs. Measures of return that should be included are dividend or interest yield, total return on investment, and internal rate of return. In addition, the actual gains or losses should be segmented into interest or dividend income, income or loss from any sales, and unrealized gains or losses. All of this information can easily be produced as a byproduct from any well designed software program.

- **Analyzing the Portfolio**

     The proactive investor will need to know not only the performance of each individual holding but also the performance by asset class. The analysis is a means of identifying potential risks as well as opportunities for improvement in the portfolio. Its purpose is to identify asset allocation and diversification issues.

     The assets in the portfolio should be classified into Cash, Certificates of Deposit, Fixed Income, Large Capitalization Equity, Small Capitalization Equity, and International Equity. This actual allocation should be compared against the benchmark or target allocation that had been established. If there is a significant deviation from the target allocation, then the portfolio should be examined for potential rebalancing.

     The value of equity holdings can be classified according to the Standard and Poor's Global Industry Classification Standards (GICS) sectors and compared to the sector weights of the S&P 500. Significant over exposure to individual sectors may indicate the need to diversify. At the end of 2005, the Financial sector accounted for 21.2 percent of the value of the S&P 500. A portfolio that had 40 percent of its value invested in the Financial sector would be a candidate for rebalancing.

     The value of each holding within the portfolio should be analyzed to see if one or more assets account for a disproportionate percentage of the portfolio's value. One should not be surprised to learn that 20 percent of the assets can often account for 80 percent of the value of the portfolio. However, if the value of one stock exceeds 20 percent of the value of the portfolio, then an assessment should be performed to determine if reducing that position might be warranted.

- **Periodic Assessments of Progress against Benchmarks**

     Unlike the professional traders, the disciplined investor does not need to monitor the performance of his/her portfolio on a real time basis. However, the disciplined investor does not let his/her portfolio go unmonitored. Investments in index funds should be monitored on a quarterly basis. Investments in individual stocks should be monitored on a weekly or monthly basis. On a daily basis, the disciplined investor will keep apprised of geopolitical and economic factors that might affect his/her current and potential holdings. Being aware of emerging trends can be a valuable asset in making profitable investment decisions.

- **Schedule of Interest and Dividend Payments**
  Knowing when a dividend or interest payment is scheduled to occur is an integral part of an effective investment management discipline. These payments can be used for reinvestment, to provide income during the retirement years or in times of financial need.
- **Listings of Maturity Dates**
  Knowing when particular fixed income investments mature is an important part of managing an investment portfolio. It allows investors to minimize idle funds, i.e., funds not earning interest, and to utilize funds to finance retirement needs.
- **Exposure to Limits of FDIC Protection**
  Any investment in a Certificate of Deposit or any other account at a bank must be covered by the Federal Deposit Insurance Corporation (FDIC) for it to be a risk free investment. Since there is a limit to the amount of protection for a depositor in an individual bank, it behooves the investor to ensure that he/she does exceed the maximum amount protected by the FDIC.

KEY TAKEAWAYS

1. **Inflation is a Force to be Reckoned with**

    The deleterious impact of inflation cannot be over emphasized. Even at low rates of inflation the degradation in purchasing power can be quite substantial given enough time. If one looks over a thirty year period of time a dollar would lose 26 percent of its purchasing power at a 1 percent annual rate of inflation; 45 percent at 2 percent; 60 percent at 3 percent; 71 percent at 4 percent; 79 percent at 5 percent; and 96 percent of its purchasing power at annual rate of inflation of 10 percent.

    There are many who will be fortunate to live into their nineties, which means they will be in retirement for thirty years. If they started saving for their retirements at age twenty five, it would mean that each dollar invested at that time would be impacted by inflation for seventy years (forty years of investment from age twenty five to sixty five and thirty years of retirement from sixty five to ninety five). That dollar invested at age twenty five would be worth after those seventy years $0.49 at 1 percent annual inflation, $0.24 at 2 percent, and $0.12 at 3 percent annual inflation.

    To put this in perspective, inflation averaged 3.99 percent per year from 1914 to 2005. This means that in 10 years a dollar would be worth $0.66, in 20 years $0.44, 30 years $0.29, 40 years $0.20 and $0.06 in seventy years.

INFLATION'S IMPACT ON PURCHASING POWER

	1%	2%	3%	4%	5%	6%	7%	8%	9%	10%
0 yrs	$1.00	$1.00	$1.00	$1.00	$1.00	$1.00	$1.00	$1.00	$1.00	$1.00
5 yrs	0.95	0.90	0.86	0.82	0.77	0.73	0.70	0.66	0.62	0.59
10 yrs	0.90	0.82	0.74	0.66	0.60	0.54	0.48	0.43	0.39	0.35
15 yrs	0.86	0.74	0.63	0.54	0.46	0.40	0.34	0.29	0.24	0.21
20 yrs	0.82	0.67	0.54	0.44	0.36	0.29	0.23	0.19	0.15	0.12
25 yrs	0.78	0.60	0.47	0.36	0.28	0.21	0.16	0.12	0.09	0.07
30 yrs	0.74	0.55	0.40	0.29	0.21	0.16	0.11	0.08	0.06	0.04
35 yrs	0.70	0.49	0.34	0.24	0.17	0.11	0.08	0.05	0.04	0.03
40 yrs	0.67	0.45	0.30	0.20	0.13	0.08	0.05	0.04	0.02	0.01
45 yrs	0.64	0.40	0.25	0.16	0.10	0.06	0.04	0.02	0.01	0.01
50 yrs	0.61	0.36	0.22	0.13	0.08	0.05	0.03	0.02	0.01	0.01
55 yrs	0.58	0.33	0.19	0.11	0.06	0.03	0.02	0.01	0.01	0.00
60 yrs	0.55	0.30	0.16	0.09	0.05	0.02	0.01	0.01	0.00	0.00
65 yrs	0.52	0.27	0.14	0.07	0.04	0.02	0.01	0.00	0.00	0.00
70 yrs	0.49	0.24	0.12	0.06	0.03	0.01	0.01	0.00	0.00	0.00

In determining the rate of inflation that might be encountered during an investors planning horizon, an examination of the distribution of rates of inflation from 1928–2005, a period of time that included periods of deflation and inflation, would be helpful. During that time, 19.2 percent of the time the annual rate of inflation was at least 1 percent; 34.6 percent at least 2 percent; 51.3 percent at least 3 percent; 70.5 percent at least 4 percent; and 78.2 percent of the time the annual rate of inflation was at least 5 percent.

2. **Don't Hitch You Career and Retirement to the Same Company**

Working for a publicly traded company no matter how large or profitable it may be involves risk. At any time, the company may decide to terminate you despite the outstanding contributions you might have made. If the company's financial situation has deteriorated, it is inevitable that it will be reflected in its stock price.

If you are in the early stages of your career, then this will most likely be a bump, albeit a painful one, in your road to success. However, if you are approaching retirement, that bump in the road can be an avalanche. You have lost your source of income and may not be able to find employment at any salary. In addition, the value of the retirement fund had it consisted of stock in your former employer would be severely reduced. In extreme cases such as Enron, the value of your retirement fund could become worthless.

The disciplined investor, no matter how promising his employer's prospects, should never have more than 10 to 15 percent of his/her retirement assets in his/her employer's stock. This provides protection from losing the funds needed for retirement.

3. **Plan Your Retirement Early**

How to plan to for retirement is not an easy task. However, it must be undertaken well in advance of actual retirement. In order to determine how much money will be needed, the retirement lifestyle must be defined. If retirement is going to be spent on extensive traveling, vacation homes, or expensive hobbies it will require more money than moving to an area with lower costs of living. Retiring at sixty two or seventy can also greatly influence the amount of money both available for and needed for retirement.

As a general rule of planning, assume you will need more and plan on living on less.

4. **Investing for Your Future is a Marathon not a Sprint**

Those born in the second half of the twentieth century have lived in a far more benign environment than their parents and grandparents, many of whom suffered through two world wars and the Great Depression. They have come to expect results in shorter timeframes than their elders. They are far more optimistic about their ability to get what they want, when they want it, and without sacrifice. Just as the microwave oven allows them to heat their food in far less time than the gas and electric ovens used by prior generations, they believe they can achieve their financial goals in the space of unrealistic, by historical standards, time frames. Furthermore, many of them believe that they can achieve returns on their investments that are unsupportable by historical norms. They tend to rationalize their perspective with the mantra "This Time is Different." They tend to avoid creating a financial safety net for themselves and defer even considering the need to save for their retirement.

Let us use the following example to illustrate the point. Assume that a person earned the median household income in 2005 of $46,326 (*source: US Census Bureau*) and was able to invest $2,500 per year (5.4 percent of his/her income) with the objective of having $500,000 at retirement. Assuming an annual rate of return of 7.5 percent, it would take 37.3 years to reach his/her objective; at 10.0 percent it would take 30.9 years and at 15.0 percent it would take 23.6 years. If one had only ten years to achieve his/her objective, it would take an annual rate of return of over 50 percent to achieve the same objective.

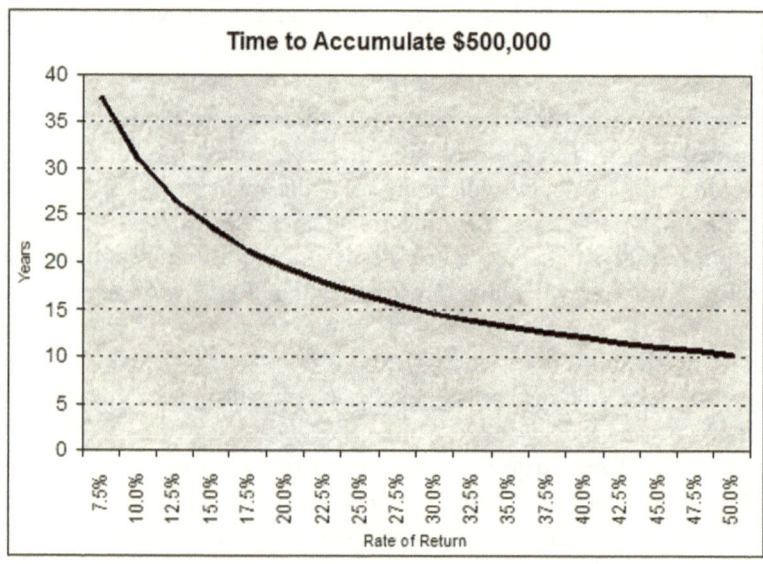

Fig. 7-1 Chart showing how many years it would take for annual investments of $2,500 to be worth $500.00 for a given annual rate of return

An analysis of the returns of the various classes of equity investments previously discussed in this book reveals how realistic it is to assume a given rate of return in developing a retirement investment strategy. There is a 56.4 percent to 62.8 percent probability of achieving at least a 7.5 percent rate of return in a particular year; 53.8 percent to 60.3 percent of a 10.0 percent rate of return; 43.6 percent to 53.8 percent of a 15.0 percent return. The probability of achieving a 50.0 percent rate of return in a single year is 1.3 percent to 14.1 percent; 0.02 percent to 2.0 percent in any two years. The probability of an investor who delays until he has only 10 years to achieve the goal of amassing $500,000 by investing $2,500 per year at a rate of return of 50.0 percent is essentially ZERO.

DISTRIBUTION of EQUITY INVESTMENT RETURNS (1928–2005)			
Rate of Return	**CUMULATIVE PROBABILITY**		
	Minimum	Average	Maximum
0.0%	65.4%	70.0%	73.1%
2.5%	61.5%	67.2%	70.5%
5.0%	60.3%	64.1%	67.9%
7.5%	56.4%	59.2%	62.8%
10.0%	53.8%	56.4%	60.3%
12.5%	50.0%	53.3%	57.7%
15.0%	43.6%	49.5%	53.8%
17.5%	39.7%	46.4%	51.3%
20.0%	35.9%	40.5%	48.7%
22.5%	30.8%	35.4%	43.6%
25.0%	26.9%	31.5%	38.5%
27.5%	23.1%	27.9%	35.9%
30.0%	20.5%	25.4%	32.1%
32.5%	12.8%	20.8%	29.5%
35.0%	10.3%	17.7%	29.5%
37.5%	6.4%	14.9%	26.9%
40.0%	6.4%	13.6%	23.1%
42.5%	5.1%	11.3%	17.9%
45.0%	2.6%	9.7%	17.9%
47.5%	1.3%	8.7%	16.7%
50.0%	1.3%	7.2%	14.1%
Data:	*Barra*		

Those who religiously save for thirty five to forty or more years would be running a marathon to achieve their retirement savings objective; those who have only twenty to thirty five years a half marathon; those with ten to twenty years the mile; and those with five to ten years a fifty yard dash. Whether your retirement is dependent on running at a relatively leisurely pace of the marathon (investing in relatively conservative investments) or the frenetic pace of the fifty yard dash (speculating in highly aggressive bets) is a matter of personal choice.

As in life, there are no sure things in investing. However, one thing is certain. The more time one has to reach a financial objective the higher the probability of success.

5.   **Concentrate on the Controllable Retirement Savings Variables**

In formulating a retirement savings strategy, there are a finite number of variables that can influence the outcome. Unfortunately, they are not all under our control. The factors that we have the most control over are when we will start saving, how much we will save, and where we will invest our savings. The factors that we have moderate control over are when we will retire and our standard of living during retirement. The factors that we have the least control over are the rates of return our retirement savings will generate and the impact of inflation on the costs of retirement.

6.   **Take Advantage of Subsidized Retirement Savings Opportunities**

Many employers offer matching contributions in their defined contribution savings plans. Typically, they will match a certain percentage of the amount contributed by their employees. Employees should consider these contributions by their employers as a safety net not an excuse to reduce the amount they save each year. Those pursuing the Possible Retirement Strategy of saving 10 percent of their annual salary and having employers that will contribute an additional 3 percent in matching funds would have to earn only 10.5 percent rather than the 12 percent assumed in this strategy in order to achieve their retirement objectives.

Another form of subsidy available to those saving for retirement are Individual Retirement Accounts (IRAs) that provide certain tax advantages.

The disciplined investor will try to take advantage of all the incentives available to him/her in saving for retirement.

7.   **Don't Invest Beyond Your Capability**

Those setting out on their investment voyage should not invest in alternatives they don't understand. Since making an investment in equities can be daunting to the novice investor, he/she would be best served by initially investing in low cost S&P 500 Index Mutual Funds or Exchange Traded Funds.

Remember the importance of diversification. A broad based index fund such as one linked to the S&P 500 are more diversified than most individuals can ever hope to be. Investors should use these vehicles as the primary tools in which to build their retirement resources.

The next logical progression would be to invest in more focused equity funds such as Large Capitalization, Small Capitalization, Growth, Value, International, or Sector Indexed Mutual Funds or Exchange Traded Funds.

Investments in individual stocks can produce higher returns or substantial losses. Disciplined investors should never predicate achieving their retirement goals on their stock picking prowess. Success at picking individual stocks is difficult enough for the professional investor. For the rest of us, investing in individual stocks should be considered as incremental savings that requires staying abreast of events that might impact our holdings.

If opportunities to invest in individual stocks arise, only after careful research and analysis should one buy.

8. **Following the Conventional Wisdom can be Expensive**

When the pundits and market gurus all share the same view, it is highly unlikely that there are opportunities to profit from their advice. The market tends to incorporate the prevailing sentiment into the price it assigns to a stock on any given day. Beware when you hear people say this time is different as they try to rationalize historically abnormal valuations.

Recognizing that as a disciplined investor you are interested in long term performance, investing in stocks that are out of favor due to short term concerns can be a highly profitable strategy to pursue. However, identifying such opportunities is not easy. It requires hard work. Opportunities for profits are often greatest when actual conditions seem gloomiest..

9. **Manage Your Exposure to Risk**

All investments, no matter how well conceived, can lose money. However, there are ways of making a potentially bad decision even worse. Investing all your money in a single stock, no matter how attractive its prospects, is something that a disciplined investor never would do. Similarly, he/she would not buy on margin.

The most dangerous of all actions one could take is to become involved in naked shorts. Naked shorting refers to selling stocks that you do not own in the expectation of being able to buy the stocks at a lower price. The reason this is so risky is that the potential loss is infinite if the stock rises in price.

10. Compound Returns Produce Dramatic Results

Compound returns can come from two sources. In the case of a fixed income investment, it is referred to as compound interest or the interest that is earned on the interest previously received. In the case of a dividend paying equity investment, compound returns refer to the dividends and price appreciation from reinvesting those dividends. Simple returns differ from compound returns in that they are not reinvested.

An investment of $100 that earns 5 percent over forty years would be worth $300 based on a simple return; $704 based on a compound return

SIMPLE versus COMPOUND RETURNS			
Years	Simple Return	Compound Return	Difference
0	100.00	100.00	0.00
1	105.00	105.00	0.00
2	110.00	110.25	0.25
3	115.00	115.76	0.76
4	120.00	121.55	1.55
5	125.00	127.63	2.63
6	130.00	134.01	4.01
7	135.00	140.71	5.71
8	140.00	147.75	7.75
9	145.00	155.13	10.13
10	150.00	162.89	12.89
11	155.00	171.03	16.03
12	160.00	179.59	19.59
13	165.00	188.56	23.56
14	170.00	197.99	27.99
15	175.00	207.89	32.89
16	180.00	218.29	38.29
17	185.00	229.20	44.20
18	190.00	240.66	50.66
19	195.00	252.70	57.70
20	200.00	265.33	65.33

SIMPLE versus COMPOUND RETURNS			
Years	Simple Return	Compound Return	Difference
21	205.00	278.60	73.60
22	210.00	292.53	82.53
23	215.00	307.15	92.15
24	220.00	322.51	102.51
25	225.00	338.64	113.64
26	230.00	355.57	125.57
27	235.00	373.35	138.35
28	240.00	392.01	152.01
29	245.00	411.61	166.61
30	250.00	432.19	182.19
31	255.00	453.80	198.80
32	260.00	476.49	216.49
33	265.00	500.32	235.32
34	270.00	525.33	255.33
35	275.00	551.60	276.60
36	280.00	579.18	299.18
37	285.00	608.14	323.14
38	290.00	638.55	348.55
39	295.00	670.48	375.48
40	300.00	704.00	404.00

The impact of compounding with equity investments can have a profound impact over the life of the investment. After forty years, a $100 initial investment in a stock paying a 5 percent annual dividend would become $704 if there was no price appreciation over the span of the investment; $1,029 at 1 percent appreciation; $1,497 at 2 percent; $2,172 at 3 percent; $3,141 at 4 percent; and $4,526 at 5 percent. When investing in dividend paying stocks, the impact of dividend reinvestment is too powerful to ignore. Substantial returns can be achieved even when there is modest price appreciation in the price of the stock. Stocks in companies that have a history of regularly increasing their dividend rates can produce even more dramatic returns than the one in this example.

	IMPACT of DIVIDEND REINVESTMENT					
	Annual Rate of Appreciation					
Years	0%	1%	2%	3%	4%	5%
0	100	100	100	100	100	100
1	105	106	107	108	109	110
2	110	112	114	117	119	121
3	116	119	123	126	130	133
4	122	126	131	136	141	146
5	128	134	140	147	154	161
6	134	142	150	159	168	177
7	141	150	161	171	183	195
8	148	159	172	185	199	214
9	155	169	184	200	217	236
10	163	179	197	216	237	259
11	171	190	210	233	258	285
12	180	201	225	252	281	314
13	189	213	241	272	307	345
14	198	226	258	294	334	380
15	208	240	276	317	364	418
16	218	254	295	343	397	460
17	229	269	316	370	433	505
18	241	285	338	400	472	556
19	253	303	362	432	514	612
20	265	321	387	466	560	673
21	279	340	414	503	611	740
22	293	360	443	544	666	814
23	307	382	474	587	726	895
24	323	405	507	634	791	985
25	339	429	543	685	862	1,083
26	356	455	581	740	940	1,192
27	373	482	621	799	1,025	1,311
28	392	511	665	863	1,117	1,442
29	412	542	711	932	1,217	1,586

IMPACT of DIVIDEND REINVESTMENT						
	Annual Rate of Appreciation					
Years	0%	1%	2%	3%	4%	5%
30	432	574	761	1,006	1,327	1,745
31	454	609	815	1,087	1,446	1,919
32	476	645	872	1,174	1,576	2,111
33	500	684	933	1,268	1,718	2,323
34	525	725	998	1,369	1,873	2,555
35	552	769	1,068	1,479	2,041	2,810
36	579	815	1,142	1,597	2,225	3,091
37	608	864	1,222	1,725	2,425	3,400
38	639	915	1,308	1,863	2,644	3,740
39	670	970	1,399	2,012	2,882	4,114
40	704	1,029	1,497	2,172	3,141	4,526

11. **Safety of Fixed Income Investments Comes at a Price**
     Fixed income investments are excellent vehicles for protecting principal
and generating income. However, they are not terribly effective in generating even reasonable growth. The following chart shows that based on returns
from fixed income investments for the years 1928 to 2005, there is a 56.2
percent to 64.1 percent probability of achieving a return on investment of
at least 2.5 percent in a given year; 34.6 percent to 42.5 percent of a 5.0
percent return; 5.1 percent to 23.3 percent of a 10.0 percent return; and 0.0
percent to 16.4 percent of a 15.0 percent return.

DISTRIBUTION of FIXED INCOME RETURNS (1928–2005)			
Rate of Return	**CUMULATIVE PROBABILITY**		
	Minimum	Average	Maximum
0.00%	71.2%	85.3%	94.9%
2.50%	56.2%	59.7%	64.1%
5.00%	34.6%	38.9%	42.5%
7.50%	12.8%	22.8%	28.8%
10.00%	5.1%	15.0%	23.3%
12.50%	1.3%	11.6%	20.5%
15.00%	0.0%	8.0%	16.4%
17.50%	0.0%	4.5%	11.0%
20.00%	0.0%	3.1%	6.8%
22.50%	0.0%	2.3%	5.5%
25.00%	0.0%	1.8%	4.1%
27.50%	0.0%	1.8%	4.1%
30.00%	0.0%	1.4%	4.1%
32.50%	0.0%	0.5%	1.4%
35.00%	0.0%	0.5%	1.4%
37.50%	0.0%	0.5%	1.4%
40.00%	0.0%	0.5%	1.4%
42.50%	0.0%	0.0%	0.0%
45.00%	0.0%	0.0%	0.0%
47.50%	0.0%	0.0%	0.0%
50.00%	0.0%	0.0%	0.0%
Data: *Barra*			

While fixed income investments have a higher probability of earning a positive annual rate of return than equity investments, the same cannot be said for their having an advantage over equities in growing an investor's capital. Those whose investment objectives require annual returns in excess of 2.5 percent would best be served by investing in equities rather than fixed income over the long term. There may be occasions when fixed income provides higher returns. In such cases, investors wishing to capitalize on such an opportunity should be sure that the Treasury or CD investments have a call protection feature.

	Cumulative Probability		
Rate of Return	Fixed Income	Equity	Difference
0.0%	85.3%	70.0%	15.3%
2.5%	59.7%	67.2%	-7.5%
5.0%	38.9%	64.1%	-25.2%
7.5%	22.8%	59.2%	-36.4%
10.0%	15.0%	56.4%	-41.4%
12.5%	11.6%	53.3%	-41.7%
15.0%	8.0%	49.5%	-41.5%
17.5%	4.5%	46.4%	-41.9%
20.0%	3.1%	40.5%	-37.4%
22.5%	2.3%	35.4%	-33.1%
25.0%	1.8%	31.5%	-29.7%
27.5%	1.8%	27.9%	-26.1%
30.0%	1.4%	25.4%	-24.0%
32.5%	0.5%	20.8%	-20.3%
35.0%	0.5%	17.7%	-17.2%
37.5%	0.5%	14.9%	-14.4%
40.0%	0.5%	13.6%	-13.1%
42.5%	0.0%	11.3%	-11.3%
45.0%	0.0%	9.7%	-9.7%
47.5%	0.0%	8.7%	-8.7%
50.0%	0.0%	7.2%	-7.2%

Investors find that equities had a 36.4 percent higher probability than fixed income of achieving at least a 7.5 percent annual rate of return; 41.4 percent of a 10.0 percent return; and 48.7 percent of a 15.0 percent return. **FIXED INCOME versus EQUITY RETURNS (1928–2005)**

Data: *Barra*

12. **Maintain a Margin of Safety**
    ALWAYS PROTECT YOURSELF FROM THE UNEXPECTED.
Just as one needs health insurance to protect against the high costs of medical care, one also needs a safety net to protect against a loss of income and to provide sufficient funds to last throughout the retirement years. It is best to save more rather than less as there will inevitably be unforeseen circumstances that will require dipping into your savings.

Monitor your investment program and ensure that you are on track to satisfy your goals. When possible, allocate a portion of any windfall to increasing your savings. A dollar saved today is more valuable than a dollar saved tomorrow.

FINAL THOUGHTS

The thought of having to plan for retirement before one has established his career direction can be a daunting task. A person often can't satisfy his/her more near term goals let alone plan for something that is twenty, thirty, forty or more years away. The intent of this book is not to scare the reader but to inform the reader of the need to save and to prioritize current needs against more distant ones.

One cannot establish a viable retirement strategy without a viable career strategy. Unless your career allows you to earn a sufficient income stream, you will have trouble supporting your life's needs and find it impossible to save for retirement. In order to have a successful career, one must be marketable. This means that you must have a set of skills and experiences that are relevant in the marketplace. Like everything else successful careers are a function of the balance of the demands of potential employers with the skills that you can supply to them. This means recognizing the inevitability of change and constantly updating your skills. Just as the demand for the blacksmith's skills have diminished so too will many of today's skills become obsolete by technology.

Suggesting that a twenty one year old start saving 6 percent of his/her salary in many cases will not be feasible. However, that should not be an excuse for not saving anything. It is better to start saving at twenty five or thirty than at fifty five or sixty. At twenty five or thirty one can still accumulate a healthy retirement fund. However, at fifty five or sixty, saving for retirement is an almost impossible task. In many cases it will not be possible to save 6 percent of one's income. Again, something is far superior to nothing.

Remember that you are investing in your future. This means that you should not take unnecessary risks. You are looking for returns that are years away not next week or month. Don't just consider the potential rewards and ignore or underestimate the potential risks. A long term perspective, allows one to invest in temporarily out of favor vehicles whose price does not adequately reflect their long term prospects. Many of the most successful investors in history saw opportunity where others did not. Remember investing in your future is a marathon and not a fifty yard dash.

If I could give the reader one and only one piece of advice it would be to lay out a road map of specific accomplishments from a career and savings perspective with associated dates for each of them. Annually, compare your accomplishments against your road map and adjust accordingly. Unless you have that road map against which to compare results, how will you ever know that you have successfully reached the end of the journey for which you have planned?

GLOSSARY OF TERMS

Term	Meaning
A/P Accounts Payable	Money owed by a company for the goods and services provided to it by its vendors.
A/R Accounts Receivable	Money owed to a company for the goods and services provided to its customers.
Accredited Investor	See Qualified Investor
Asset Allocation	A plan for maintaining a predetermined mix of investments in different types of assets.
Asset Turnover	A measure of how efficiently a company is able to use its assets in generating revenues. Asset Turnover is defined as Revenues divided by Total Assets.
Basis Point	One one hundredth (0.01) of a percent
Bear	Someone with a pessimistic view of a stock or market
Beta	A means of quantifying the volatility of a security or portfolio of securities in comparison to the entire stock market. A Beta of: • < 1.0 indicates that a stock is less volatile than the market • = 1.0 indicates that a stock and the market have the same degree of volatility • >1.0 indicates that the stock is more volatile than the market.
Book Value	Assets minus debts
Bull	Someone with an optimistic view of a stock or market
Call Protection	A fixed income instrument that cannot be redeemed or called by the issuer prior to maturity.
Capital Spending	Expenditures by a company on assets whose useful lives exceed one year

Term	Meaning
Compound Returns	The returns generated from the reinvestment of earnings.
Continuing Operations	Those operations a company plans on keeping.
Debt/Equity Ratio	An indication of the proportion of its financing comes from debt and equity. It is defined as the ratio of long term debt to equity.
Depression	A long and severe period of declining economic output.
Dividend Coverage Ratio	This is a measurement of a company's ability to maintain its dividend payments and is the ratio of the current earnings per share to the current dividends per share
Dividend Payout Ratio	This is another measure of a company's ability to maintain its dividend. It is the inverse of the Dividend Coverage Ratio. It is defined as the ratio of the current dividend per share by the earnings per share.
Dividend Rate	The dividend amount per share of stock paid to stockholders each year.
Dividend Yield	Actual dividend paid per year divided by the value of the security
Dollar Cost Averaging	A technique that calls for investing equal amounts of money periodically rather than investing all funds at a single time
Earnings Growth Rate	A measure of how much a company's annual earnings are projected to increase
EPS Earnings per Share	The ratio of the net earnings of a company divided by the number of shares of common stock outstanding.
Earnings Yield	The amount of earnings represented by each dollar worth of stock. It is calculated by dividing earnings per share by the market price of each share.
Ex-Dividend Date	Date after which the stock trades without its dividend

Term	Meaning
Fiscal Year	The twelve month period used by a company for accounting purposes. The term is most often used when the accounting year differs from the calendar year.
Float Weighted Index	Assigning a weight in an index based on the number of shares available to be traded.
Fundamental Analysis	A method of determining a stock's price based on its intrinsic value.
Gross Domestic Product	A measure of the economic output of a country. It is the market value of the final goods and services produced within a country in a given period of time.
Gross Margin	A measure of the profitability of sales before taking into account overhead and other indirect costs. It is revenues less direct cost of sales expressed as a percentage of sales
Interest Coverage	A measure of a company's ability to pay interest on its outstanding debt. It is defined as the ratio of earnings before interest and taxes to the interest expense of its debt.
Inventory Turnover	A measure of how efficiently a company manages its inventory levels to support its sales. It is defined as the ratio of cost of goods sold divided by average inventory.
IRR **Internal rate of Return**	The interest rate that results in a net present value of zero for a stream of cash flows over time. It is the expected rate of return generated over the life of an investment

Term	Meaning
Leverage Ratio	Leverage Ratio is typically used to describe the sensitivity of changes in: • sales volume to profitability, Operating Leverage. After fixed costs have been met, relatively small changes in sales produce disproportionate changes in profitability due to the relationship between the fixed and variable costs of a company. • changes in profits to earnings per share, Financial Leverage. The higher the proportion of a company's capital structure is in long term debt, the more sensitive its earnings per share will be to incremental changes in profitability. It should be remembered that leverage can affect a company's performance both in a positive and negative way.
Limit Order	Buy order to be executed for no more than a specified price
Liquidity Ratio	A measure of a company's ability to meet its short term obligations through the use of those assets whose value is fairly certain. It is the ratio of the sum of cash, marketable securities and receivables divided by current liabilities. The Liquidity Ratio is sometimes referred to as the Acid Test.
Market Capitalization	Current price per share multiplied by the total number of shares outstanding
Market Order	Buy or sell order to be executed at the current market price
Market Weighted Index	Assigning a weight in an index based on the market value of a company's shares outstanding.
Net Profit Margin	A measure of the profitability of a company in terms of its ability to transform each sales dollar into profits. It is defined as net profits as a percentage of sales.

Term	Meaning
Operating Profit	Amount of profit a company earns from the sales of its products and services before taking into consideration other sources of income, financing costs and taxes.
Pareto Principle (80:20 Rule)	Also known as the 80:20 Rule states that that for many phenomena, 80 percent of the consequences stem from 20 percent of the causes
Ponzi Scheme	A scheme that involves paying abnormally high returns to investors out of the money paid in by subsequent investors.
Payables	See Accounts Payable
Present Value	A technique for calculating what a amount of money at some future date is worth in current day's dollars
Pre-Tax Margin	The profitability of a company's income after accounting for all sources of income and expenses except for income taxes. It is presented as a percentage of revenues.
Price to Book Ratio	The ratio of a company's stock price per share divided by its book value per share (assets minus debt divided by the number of shares outstanding)
Price to Cash Flow	The market price of the stock divided by the cash flow per share (earnings per share plus depreciation per share)
PEG Price to Earnings Growth	The ratio of a stock's Price-Earnings Ratio (P/E) to its annual growth in Earning per Share (EPS)
P/E Price to Earnings Ratio	The ratio of the market price of a stock divided by its earnings per share
Price to Sales Ratio	The ratio of a company's price per share to its sales per share
Qualified Investor	A financially sophisticated investor who needs reduced protection. This is an investor whose income and investable assets exceed a specified amount of money.
Quick Ratio	See Liquidity Ratio

Term	Meaning
Receivables	See Accounts Receivable
Receivables Turnover	An accounting measure of how effectively a company collects on the sales to customers to whom it has extended credit. It is the ratio of Net Credit Sales to Average Accounts Receivable.
Recession	A fall in a country's Gross Domestic Product (GDP) that lasts for two or more successive quarters
Reversion to the Mean	A theory stating that equities market will return to its average valuation level.
ROA **Return on Assets**	A measure of how profitably a company utilizes its assets. It is the ratio of net profits divided by total assets
ROE **Return on Equity**	Net profits expressed as a percentage of stockholders' equity
ROI **Return on Invested Capital**	A measure of the how well a company utilized its capital (debt plus equity). It is the ratio of a company's earnings to its invested capital.
Reversion to the Mean	A concept that a series of values will tend to return to their average value. These values could be Returns on Equity, Price to Book Ratio, Price to Earnings Ratio, etc.
S&P 500	A list compiled by Standard & Poor's, a financial research and analysis organization, of the 500 largest United States corporations based on market capitalization.
Short Interest Ratio	It is the number of days it will take short sellers to cover their positions in the event that the company's stock rises in price. It is the ratio of the number of shares sold short to the average number of shares traded in a day. A ratio of 5.0 or more is considered a bearish indicator.
Short Interest Shares	The total number of shares of stock sold short as a percentage of the total number of shares outstanding.

Term	Meaning
Short Sale	The selling of shares which have been borrowed in the expectation of buying them at a lower price in the future at which time the borrowed shares would be returned,
Stock Split	The division of the existing number of the outstanding shares of a company into multiple shares. Since the price per share is adjusted for the split, the total value of the shares does not change.
Stop Order	Order to sell a stock if it should drop below a specified price
Technical Analysis	Utilization of charts and other analytical tools to analyze historical stocks prices and trading volumes to determine future stock prices irrespective of a stock's intrinsic value.
TIPS	Treasury Inflation Protected Security
TIPS Spread	The difference in yield between the nominal and inflation-indexed securities with same maturities. The TIPS spread is indicative of the average rate of inflation expected over the maturity of the security.
Treasury Bills	Obligations of the US Treasury that mature in less than one year
Treasury Bonds	Obligations of the US Treasury that mature in ten to thirty years
Treasury Notes	Obligations of the US Treasury that mature in two to ten years
Total Operations	The inclusion of discontinued operations in the determination of a company's performance.

BIBLIOGRAPHY

About.com

Barra

Barron's

Bureau of Labor Statistics

Business Week

Census.gov

Columbia Encyclopedia. Sixth Edition 2001

Congressional Research Service *Current Population Survey*

Equitymaster.com

Federal Reserve

Federal Reserve Board *Survey of Consumer Finances.* 2004

Forbes

Fortune

FRED (Federal Reserve Database in St. Louis)

Gummy-stuff.com

Helfert, Erich A. *Techniques of Financial Analysis.*
Richard D. Irwin, Inc. 1963

Indexfunds.com

Inflationdata.com

Investopedia.com

Investorguide.com
Lievegoed, Bernard *Phases of Childhood*
Anthroposophic Press 1987

Mathworld.wolfram.com

Monthly Labor Review, January 2006

Morningstar.com
Motley Fool
Retirement Confidence Survey 2005

Ricardo, David. *The Principles of Political Economy and Taxation.* 1817

Schumpeter, Joseph *Capitalism, Socialism, and Democracy* 1942

Smith, Adam *An Inquiry into the Nature and Causes of the Wealth of Nations.* 1776

Standard & Poor's

Street Authority

StreetAuthority.com

The Frank Russell Company

Time Magazine *Modern Inventions of the Years 2000–2004*

United States Department of Energy

US Census Bureau

Victorianweb.com

Wall Street Journal

Yahoo Finance

INDEX

ABOUT THE AUTHOR

The author has been an avid investor since his early teens. During the course of his lifetime he has developed a philosophy that has served him in his own professional development and in the creation of an investment portfolio for his family's financial needs.

His perspectives have been developed from his lifelong study of investing, his actual experiences as a registered representative, an individual investor, as well as from working for large companies in industry and as a management consultant to Fortune 500 companies.

Mr. Doniger received a Masters in Business Administration from Columbia University Graduate School of Business and a Bachelor of Science Degree in Mechanical Engineering from Tufts University. He has taught undergraduate and graduate level courses in production control, inventory management, information technology and finance at Fitchburg State College and Webster University.

978-0-595-48465-2
0-595-48465-4